zen
and the
art of
screenwriting

zen and the art of screenwriting

insights and interviews

William Froug

SILMAN-JAMES PRESS   LOS ANGELES

First Edition
10 9 8 7 6 5 4 3 2 1

Library of Congress Cataloging-in-Publication Data

Froug, William.
Zen and the art of screenwriting : insights and interviews /
Willian Froug. — 1st ed.
1. Motion picture authorship. 2. Screenwriters—Interviews.
I. Title
PN1996.F776 1996   808.2'3—dc20   96-43387

ISBN: 1-879505-31-2

Cover design by Wade Lageose, Art Hotel

Printed and bound in the United States of America

Silman-James Press
1181 Angelo Drive
Beverly Hills, CA 90210

To the writers of original screenplays who create the stories, the characters, the scenes, the dialogues, the structures, and the themes—everything you see on the screen. They are the true and only authors (*auteurs*, for you lovers of French) of the films they conceive. And thanks to the many talented people who help *interpret the screenwriter's vision.*

At its simplest and most profound level, Zen is purely devoted to liberating the hidden potential of the human mind.
—Thomas Cleary, *Zen Essence*

Contents

Preface   *xi*

Acknowledgments   *xv*

What's the Big Idea?   *3*

Which Is It?   *14*

What's Going On? Don't Tell Me   *20*

New Big Talent on the Block:

    An Interview with Frank Darabont   *27*

A Heart as Big as the Ritz:

    An Interview with Bo Goldman   *49*

Fake It Till You Make It   *65*

The Movie Game   *74*

How to Get There from Here   *84*

Sometimes a Really Great Notion:

    An Interview with Callie Khouri   *89*

A World-Class Thoroughbred, a Sure Winner:

    An Interview with Eric Roth   *109*

You Gotta Have It   *131*

What Will Happen Next?   *133*

Rewrite Is Might   *145*

Peoples Who Need Peoples:

An Interview with David and Janet Peoples   *153*

Promises, Promises!   *183*

Another Road, a Different Journey   *190*

The Butcher Who Minted Millions   *199*

A Gentle, Shy, Modest Lady with a Powerful Pen:

An Interview with Ruth Prawer Jhabvala   *209*

A Screenwriter's Worst Nightmares:

An Interview with Laurence Dworet   *225*

Hunting Big Game   *253*

Batter Up!   *257*

Don't Call Me, and I Won't Call You   *263*

Dying is Easy, Comedy is Hard:

An Interview with Larry Gelbart   *269*

"Stronger Than Fiction" by Larry Gelbart   *281*

A Writer for All Seasons and All Reasons:

An Interview with Stuart Kaminsky   *289*

Five Queasy Pieces   *315*

You're Never Too Young   *323*

To Market, To Market   *330*

Preface

One day many years ago, this sentence popped into my head: "Anybody who looks at dead bodies often enough is bound to get tired of it sooner or later."

I took out my little black Royal portable typewriter and put that sentence down on paper. That's all I had, but I kept adding sentences. The second sentence told me that my narrator was a private detective, and a story gradually developed from there. I had no idea where it would lead me—no outline, no plan of any kind. Just this process of one word, one sentence followed by another word, another sentence and another until 15,000 words and about 250 pages later, I had a mystery novel or novella, as it's called.

My former college roommate, E. Jack Neuman, was already a professional writer in Hollywood, so I sent it to him for evaluation. He wrote back that he liked it and asked if I would like him to give my manuscript to a book publishing agent. I replied, "Are you kidding?"

The book agent liked my tale but said it was too short for hardcover. However, he gave it to another agent, Captain Joseph T. Shaw, former editor of the famous *Black Mask* magazine, who wrote me that I was the next Raymond Chandler or Dashiell Hammett, both of whom had started their careers in pulp magazines. He said he had been their agent, and that he would sell my novella immediately to a top pulp magazine, which he did. As you know, I did not become the next Chandler or Hammet, but $300 in 1946 was a fortune to a very young, former subchaser skipper only a few weeks back from the distant atolls of the mid-Pacific.

My professional writing career was launched, all because a sentence popped into my head and I sat down at my little portable typewriter and kept pounding away every day, one sentence at a time, until I discovered I'd told a good story that I myself hadn't known.

I tell you this to both explain and support my thesis that all of us have stories buried inside us, and that the single most important thing you must do is write your ideas down as quickly as possible, putting one word after the next and so on. If you stick to it, surprisingly soon you'll have a screenplay, a novel, a poem, or whatever you chose. (It's the magic of freeing your unconscious mind, letting your ideas flow and going where they take you.)

It's the way every writer in history has launched his or her career. It's hard work, but it's also a great pleasure and source of joy. And the best part is that we can all do it, some more successfully than others, it's true. But we can all put a word on a page, follow it with another word and another, and see how our lives are forever changed.

Acknowledgments

To my great and good friend Stuart Kaminsky, who welcomed me to Sarasota almost three years ago with a warmth and ongoing friendship that has made this writer feel right at home; to marvelous Mary Fox, who guided me through the treacherous jungles of computerland and without whom this book would be completed by the year 2096, maybe; to Andrew Froug, the youngest and most promising writer of our little clan; and Emily Froug, future queen and present princess; to Ashley Hirano, the bright young star of future Hawaiian poets; and especially to my children, who have stood by me through very dark times yet remain my loyal and loving friends: Suzy Allegra, Nancy Earth, Lisa Froug-Hirano, and Jonathan Froug, each my life's enduring treasure; and a special thanks to the greatest editor it's been my joy to encounter, Jim Fox, who has given me unconditional support lo these past five years and four books. Without Jim's diligent research, our quotations might have been thinner than lice on a billiard ball. And thanks, too, to Jim's partner, the redoubtable Gwen Feldman. A lifetime of gratitude to E. Jack Neuman, my first mentor who guided a sailor home from the sea into a lifelong writing career. Fifty years of friendship and encouragement. A special bow to that stalwart band of liars, the Writers' Friday Liar's Poker mini-mob, villains and scoundrels all: Joe Hayes, Rob Roy Buckingham, Bill Guisewite, Wayne Barcomb, Peter King, Walt Cannon, Jules Koslow, Walt Kempley, Jack Garside, Milton Gurvitz, Stuart Kaminsky, Paul Moser, and Liar-in-Chief Tim Kantor. These distinguished gentlemen make a writer's lonely life a happier experience with weekly doses of outrageous and robust humor. Bless them all: Tony winners, Emmy winners, Edgar winners, Pulitzer Prize winners, and just plain ink-stained wretches who are all winners; and thanks to Sean Castello of the Writers Guild of America, west, for diligent research. And last, but actually first and foremost, the glorious light of my life these past dozen years, my best friend, companion, lover, wife, in-house superstar, first and toughest editor, and spectacular human being, Christine Michaels, without whom not only my pages but my life would be blank.

With Gratitude beyond measure.

W.F.

Sarasota, Fl.

5/26/96

Coleridge was a drug addict. Poe was an alcoholic. Marlowe was killed by a man whom he was treacherously trying to stab. Pope took money to keep a woman's name out of a satire, then wrote a piece so that she could still be recognized anyhow. Chatterton killed himself. Byron was accused of incest. Do you still want to be a writer—and if so, why?
—Bennett Cerf, *Shake Well Before Using*

The words "Kiss Kiss Bang Bang," which I saw on an Italian movie poster, are perhaps the briefest statement imaginable of the basic appeal of movies.
—Pauline Kael, *Kiss Kiss Bang Bang*

Writing is nothing more than a guided dream.
—Jorge Luis Borges, *Doctor Brodie's Report*

What's the Big Idea?

"Before you have even written the screenplay, you have determined the success or failure of the film simply in your choice of what to write about. At that moment the die is cast."
—Walter Brown Newman,
The Screenwriter Looks at the Screenwriter

"The head of a major studio, speaking on condition of anonymity, said that star power is limited, and often meaningless, unless the film strikes a nerve. 'There's no justification for any of these high salaries unless you get the actor in a film with a terrific idea.'"
—Bernard Weinraub, *New York Times*

Nothing is more important to you than having a great idea *before you begin to work on your story*. A writer with a great idea, even poorly executed, can launch his or her career like a rocket, while a writer with a poor idea, no matter how brilliantly written, will probably get nowhere. As the old aphorism puts it, you can't make a silk purse out of a sow's ear.

Conventional wisdom has it that in screenwriting the idea is only five percent while execution is ninety-five percent. In my early days as a teacher, I subscribed to that theory. But in looking back on my lifetime of writing and studying screenwriting, I have come to the conclusion that the ratio is more likely the other way around.

Ideas are seeds that appear, almost magically, in your mind. Most of them do not grow, but the healthy, strong ones do. *You must write them down*. If you do not, they might very well vanish.

When you feel strongly about your idea, begin to play with it in your brain. Noodle around with it, see where it will take you—*what kind of story* it can become. Once you decide to think about possible developments, think about characters who fit your particular story, and see where these people lead you.

This period of thinking about your story *idea* is critically important. Sometimes writers spend weeks, months, or even years before they're ready to put their story together. This is the all-important incubation period—your "baby" is taking shape, getting legs, arms, and a heart: growing in the womb of your brain. Under no circumstance should you consult with anybody during this incubation time. Wait until you're certain your idea has the capacity to grow and develop. If you tell your ideas to anyone, you'll lose the energy to write them.

When you are certain you have something fresh and original, then you are ready to get serious about it. It is only then that you are ready to start making notes, putting down bits and pieces of your projected story as they occur to you. Don't rush it; take all the time you need laying it out. Begin to outline it, if you chose to. Many major screenwriters do not outline their screenplays before they write. It's a personal choice. There is no rule that says you have to outline a screenplay before you write it. Callie Khouri didn't outline *Thelma and Louise*, I.A.L. Diamond and Billy Wilder didn't outline *Some Like It Hot*. Many classic screenplays were written without an outline: *Citizen Kane* for example. (If you have an assignment to write television, producers insist on a detailed outline; you have no choice. But when you're writing on spec, write any way you please.) Most of my novelist friends outline each chapter before they begin to write, but they still feel free to strike off in a new directions if the characters or story take unexpected turns.

But we're rushing ahead. Before you even start performing mental gymnastics with your story, make sure you have an idea that really seizes you, that you are certain you want to devote a big hunk of your time to writing.

A note of caution: All too many aspiring screenwriters are

"finding their ideas" from reruns of old movies on late-night television. Sometimes you can take an old movie and try to make a new and better version of it, but more often you can't. I believe that in most cases, aspiring screenwriters aren't aware that they've unconsciously chosen familiar stories and tired situations, which professional readers will catch within minutes. I'd wager a guess that most of the submitted screenplays that wind up in wastebaskets or being returned to sender are conscious or unconscious reworkings of old movies. Most of the time, this is the road to defeat.

You will give your career a jump start if you start by writing screenplays based on your own original, fresh ideas, no matter how difficult that is. Think of David Webb Peoples' *Unforgiven*, and you see what a gifted screenwriter can do with a fresh approach to the seemingly tired Western genre. Dave dug deep, searching for the truths beneath the myths, and thus put himself into the highest rank of contemporary screenwriters.

Story is, indeed, king of the jungle, *but the idea is father to the king*. What better example than Michael Crichton's *Jurassic Park*. Once Dr. Crichton hit on the idea of the rebirth of the dinosaurs, he tapped into a universal consciousness that lifted the movie into all-time worldwide box-office success. His was an idea whose time had come.

In the early '60s, while I was under contract to MGM as a writer-producer of television series, veteran screenwriter William Bowers set up a screenwriters' table at the MGM commissary and insisted all the writers on the lot meet there for lunch. Bill was trying to recreate the old glory days of MGM—in those days, the writers had their own table in the commissary, where they talked story and told insider jokes.

Here, Bill regaled us with stories about the old days in Hollywood:

"Back in the '30s, when screenwriter Bob Hopkins was under contract here, he hit on an idea that got him so excited that he rushed unannounced into Louis B. Mayer's office.

"'I've got it, L.B.,' shouted Bob, 'a hit picture, it can't miss, wait'll you hear it!'

"Mayer liked Bob, so he didn't throw him out," Bowers continued.

"'Okay,' the studio boss said skeptically, 'what's the big idea?'

"'San Francisco, 1906! The earthquake! The city totally destroyed! Clark Cable, Jeanette McDonald, Spencer Tracy! All under contract to MGM. We'll call it *San Francisco*! What a picture! Can't you just see it?'"

"'Yes, I can,' Mayer replied, smiling, 'and I'll buy it.'"

"Hopkins wrote the story and got his option picked up with a salary boost. Anita Loos, one of the best in the business, wrote the screenplay." Bowers concluded, "It's a true story; all the guy had was an idea and a title. The picture got an Oscar nomination."

Okay, now it's sixty years later, but I assure you, the only thing that has changed for screenwriters is that now you have to write the screenplay first. A hot idea is still a hot idea and still the quickest way to rocket yourself into orbit as a screenwriter. And the beauty is that, when a hot idea occurs to you, you'll know it. Here's how:

(1) *It will be an idea you have never seen before.* This is *crucial.*

(2) It will excite you so much that you *must* write it and can't wait to get started.

(3) Your instincts will convince you that it's *something the audience will feel excited about, too.*

(4) It very likely will be the easiest screenplay you have ever written because it has a clean, clear, strong *action line. One* line of action will drive the story. (This does not mean that the screenplay "will write itself." No screenplay ever wrote itself, in spite of frequent sappy assurances from producers and studio execs that it will somehow magically happen.)

A great idea will likely begin as a figment in your imagination, embryonic, undeveloped. But as you examine and reexamine it, it will grow, and as it does, you will learn exactly where it's going to go and who the characters are who will take you on your journey. Developing a great idea is among the most joyful experiences a writer can know.

I was hit by great screenplay ideas twice and sold them both in the same week. Though they remain on United Artists' huge shelves of unproduced works, selling them made for a happy and profitable year.

A great screenplay idea is a precious gift that happens to writers all too infrequently. When it does, get it down on paper as quickly as possible. Stay up all night, if need be, but get the core of it written, even if only a few scene cards. No matter how good it is, an idea tends to be ephemeral by nature; it can completely vanish by the next day, much to your sad surprise.

Original ideas have led many screenwriters to fame and fortune. Here's an example:

UCLA screenwriting student Greg Widen came up with an original idea in Richard Walter's graduate seminar. It was about a 14th-century Scotsman who apparently died in battle, only to discover that he's immortal and is still crossing swords with his enemy in 20th-century Manhattan.

You won't come across many notions that offbeat, but Greg was dedicated to it and worked hard to bring it to life. He called it *Highlander*. (Widen tells the story of the sale of that screenplay and how he went about getting an agent in *The New Screenwriter Looks at the New Screenwriter*.)

Highlander, as you probably know, became a hit picture that spawned two sequels, *Highlander II* and *Highlander III* (a rarity, indeed), and then became an animated television series. Greg opted not to write either of the sequels, but he received fat checks from each film as creator of the original characters and idea. That first, crazy, offbeat idea—*Highlander*—not only established his career as a highly successful screenwriter, it also earned him, and continues to earn him, huge sums of money. Not bad for a kid who spent ages eighteen to twenty-one as a Los Angeles fireman (which gave him the background for his second film, *Backdraft*) before moving on to college. In movies as in life, ideas resonate. And if they are well executed, they can take on a life of their own.

Nobody could know at the outset that Greg Widen's off-the-wall idea would be a big-time commercial success. He gave me *High-*

lander to read when he came into my class, and the truth is that I found it confusing and disappointing. Obviously the marketplace disagreed. It was a fresh, original idea whose time had come, and this young writer had faith in it and gave it his all.

Highlander is a sterling example of what you can do when you ignore what all the "experts" tell you is "commercial." Greg understood the most basic truth every aspiring screenwriter needs to learn: *Go with your own vision, go with what you believe in.* Your creative instincts are far more likely to bring you success than attempts to second-guess the audience or the marketplace. Nobody can do that. Studio executives are routinely fired for being unable to predict the box office.

Of course, sometimes you will have an exciting idea that turns out to be fool's gold the next morning. No matter, there will be other ideas. And here I must repeat: *Always write down the ideas that excite you.* Otherwise, there is a strong likelihood that you will forget them. A few minutes of your time could lead to a lifetime of fulfillment.

Here's how Walter Newman did it: He'd buy a stack of blue, 4x6, lined index cards, and he would jot down scraps of ideas on these cards—character names, bits of dialogue, scene ideas, whatever came into his mind that might prove relevant down the line. Gradually, he would begin to assemble these bits and pieces (often as many as 300 index cards) and work out a story as he went along. Walter told me that the story came easily after completing his "idea process."

Walter's approach was both original and unorthodox, but he wrote some classic screenplays: *The Magnificent Seven* and *The Great Escape*, among others. Alas, Walter had a short fuse in those days and if he didn't like his first viewing of the rough cut, if he felt somebody had tampered with his lines, he would storm out of the screening room demanding that his name be taken off the picture. Thus he simultaneously achieved recognition among Hollywood's cognoscenti as one of the great screenwriters of his time while maintaining his anonymity outside of the movie business. In later years, he could laugh about his early fits of temper, but they cost him a great deal of residual money as well as widespread recognition.

Remember, ideas are seeds that can grow into great screenplays, great income, and a great screenwriting career. Ideas are the coins of the realm. Treasure them, get them down on paper as soon as you can (if only in note form), respect them, work with them, and you will thereby control your own career destiny.

Birthplaces

Many writers (and I include myself) report that the best story ideas often come while they are doing something else: taking a shower, taking a long walk, trying to get to sleep at night, cooking, taking drives away from heavy traffic. The common denominator seems to be that the unconscious is the birthplace of our best ideas. They tend to pop to the surface while you are involved in routine activities that use only a minimal amount of your attention.

I suggest that if your mind seems to be lying fallow or empty of story ideas, *do not sit down and try to think of an idea.* Instead, try some relatively mindless pursuits that will take the stress off of your thought process and allow your unconscious mind to rise to the surface and rescue you.

It's like trying to remember somebody's name and repeatedly going blank, until you finally stop trying to remember. There is probably a scientific name for this phenomenon. I'll think of it after I've stopped trying to think of it.

Taking the pressure off of yourself and letting go of fear are the primary and vital conditions you need to create.

Which Is It?

Is screenwriting primarily art or craft? Current fashion dictates that craft is the be-all and end-all of screenwriting. Or, as we used to say, the three rules of screenwriting are (a) structure, (b) structure, and (c) structure.

Of course, craft and good structure are important, but they are neither the be-all nor the end-all of screenwriting. This is not a chicken-or-egg question. First comes art and only then comes craft. Eventually, in great screenplays, both are blended. However, we teachers and professional writers have emphasized structure so fervently and convincingly that structure has become the god of screenwriting. This fixation has led to a mound of look-alike screenplays that could reach to the top of Arnold Schwarznegger's bank roll. This addiction to structure *über alles* puts aspiring screenwriters into a mechanical mindset before they conceive the first idea of what they are interested in writing. And this is the most serious and deadly flaw in the non-credentialed, so-called story-structure gurus' lectures and self-serving articles and books. Teaching structure is easy; helping newcomers develop their art is difficult and time-consuming. You can't accomplish it in the fast-buck, weekend screenwriting seminars that these folk travel about the country and conduct for the rubes. (But there's always a good living to be made hustling the gullible.) These seminar hustlers, like their turn-of the-century counterparts, the snake-oil salesmen who sold elixirs they claimed would cure every disease that ailed you, sell screenwriting formulas that they claim will boost you into big-time screenwriting heaven. (It is no small paradox that few if any of these gurus have ever sold a screenplay themselves.) Just follow their 25, 32, 16, 57 easy "steps" and you've got it made. It's all about structure, so they say.

They're dead wrong. Structure (i.e., craft) follows art, not the other way around.

First comes the idea, which needs whatever time it takes to grow—sometimes weeks or months or even years. This idea-nurturing time must not be restricted by such premature questions as "How do I structure it?" Start the structuring process too soon and your idea is a heartbeat away from your wastebasket. Next comes the story. Again, this needs to be worked out free-form in your mind *before you put it in the straitjacket called "structure."* Now is *not* the time to think about where your acts go, what page such-and-such development takes place. A premature rush to structure is a good way to block further development of your idea and your story.

Only after you've become comfortable with your story idea and know you want to write it do you come to the next phase: plotting. Here is where structure—the mechanics—begins to count. Some teachers feel that you must make an outline that dots every "i" and crosses every "t." All neat and tidy. I don't agree. Art is sloppy, untidy. Assembling a car engine is neat and tidy.

Rigid outlines are the kiss of death to creativity and the joy of writing your screenplay. I believe that often during the outline phase (if you choose to use an outline), your characters will lead you to new and interesting developments. They will take you in unexpected directions that a rigid outline cannot accommodate. If they're real, vivid, living characters, they will and should offer you constant surprises, new avenues, interesting new involvements. Once you are under way, your characters (if you're really in touch with them and vice versa) write the dialogue—you don't. Give yourself plenty of breathing room, loosen up, lighten up.

If your characters take you too far afield, then do what Neil Simon says he does when his characters wander off: say, "Sorry, pal, you're in the wrong story," and start writing notes on a new pad.

But, more often than not, if your action line is clear and strong, the new journeys your characters suggest will stay within the story you want to tell, while bringing you unexpected excitement and originality.

Characters *are* story; the two are inextricably linked. And to give life to their stories, characters must have a strong voice. If they are locked into a rigid structure, your screenplay is likely to fall flat. This is precisely why so many of our greatest and most creative screenwriters eschew outlines and carefully planned structures.

Woody Allen, an outstanding example of a film artist of the highest rank, a real and rare honest-to-god American auteur, often restructures his films in the cutting room, after the movie is shot. Restructuring movies in the editing room is not an unusual practice. If the screenplays are correctly outlined and structured, why does this practice persist? Do directors and editors just like to waste their time fooling around with the film? No. Art is a process of discovery, trial and error—seeing what works and what doesn't. The only thing these post-production cutters are concerned with is telling the story. They know all the tinkering in the world *is* a waste of time *unless they protect the story.*

Scores of movies that we now think of as American masterpieces were being written and rewritten while they were filming: *Casablanca* and *Gone With the Wind*, to name just two. The list is endless. Is this because the screenplays were poorly constructed to begin with? Or is it because moviemaking is primarily an art form, involving, like all art, following your gut instincts? If something new, exciting, or better comes up while filming, the filmmakers, often in spite of budget restrictions, go with it. If these screenplays were poorly structured to begin with, why did they get made? Because they had great stories to tell. *Structure will always be secondary to story.*

Art is an act of liberation. It is the freedom to let your imagination, your Muse, create new ideas. Art offers a chance to explore the previously undiscovered, unknown domain of your subconscious. And, yes, your soul. Creativity is mysterious and often surprising.

It can seem dangerous (especially to the dogmatic) because it demands risk-taking, it defies rules and dogma. And sometimes you find yourself thinking the unthinkable. That's when you know you're on the right track.

You are first and foremost an artist and then a craftsperson. Reversing this order is dangerous to your career and, not just incidentally, can destroy your joy of writing.

What's Going On? Don't Tell Me.

The other day, while I was heading south on Highway 75, the traffic slowed to a crawl. We were moving bumper to bumper, sticking our heads out our windows trying to figure out what was holding us up. But we could not see the problem. Most of us probably assumed a heavy-duty traffic accident—ambulances, cops directing traffic, a tie-up of some magnitude. After some time, the pace gradually began to pick up and the source of the slow-down was revealed: *a guy along the roadside was changing his tire!* The attention of hundreds of drivers was held by one man changing a tire. Everyone had to slow down to get a look at what was going on.

I'm sure that an experience like this has happened to you. People are naturally curious, especially about a puzzle, a mystery. Without curiosity, there would have been no slow-down. If there actually had been an accident, police would have had to be out on the highway to make the gawkers keep moving. The bigger the accident, the more police it would have required to keep the traffic flowing. People have to know what is going on.

In the world of screenwriting, this is called creating *the need to know*. Along with surprise, the need to know is one of the most important tools the storyteller must use to hold his or her audience. It's not only "What will happen next?" that you must create in your audience's (or reader's) mind, but also *"What is happening now? What's going on?"* Every scene can and should have its own little secrets; call them mysteries.

Avoid telling your audience everything. Withheld information is worth its weight in rubies.

The next great tool every screenwriter must have in his or her toolbox is *surprise*.

A muscular, rugged, thirtyish man in a heavily stained T-shirt and jeans, his face dirty and sweat-stained, carrying an ordinary paper sack, enters an upscale jewelry shop in downtown Manhattan.

The guard at the door eyes him warily but has no reason to detain or question him: He's just a working man, probably coming from one of the construction sites down the street. But, the cop is thinking, "What's in the paper sack?"

And the audience is thinking, "What's in the sack?" and "What's this character doing in Tiffany?"

The guy looks around, surveying diamonds, pearls, expensive jewelry, then casually crosses to the nearest clerk and says quietly but firmly, "I'd like to see the manager of the store. And I'm in a hurry."

The clerk glances over to the armed guard, a bit nervous about this character. The guard merely nods; the man wants to see the manager, nothing illegal about that. But the guard's hand moves slowly toward his gun, preparing for the worst.

You've told your audience nothing, you've shown them a scene that tugs at their curiosity. Though it will not sustain for a long period of time, right now they have a *need to know what's going on*.

It's as simple as that, but it's also much more important than it seems. You're on page one of your screenplay and you've created a short-term need to know. Something odd is going on. We are curious from the moment the man enters the store carrying the paper bag (The paper bag is very important. We need to know what's inside it.)

With the simplest device in the world you've grabbed your audience and your reader's attention. The next thing is just as important for you to achieve, but tougher to accomplish. It's called: *Surprise*!

I don't know what's in the sack or why this person is in Tiffany asking to see the manager as quickly as possible. I don't even know if he's who he appears to be. And, perhaps most important of all, I need to know what's in the paper bag he's carrying. I have no idea, but I'd certainly like to know, and I certainly expect, as a screenwriting teacher and as a member of your audience, that when I find out, I'll be completely surprised. Your job is to *avoid the predictable*.

Okay, that's one illustration of how to create the need to know and set up a surprise.

Go to it. You're the screenwriter, I'm only the writer of this little exercise. Do your stuff: Who is this workman? What does he want? What's in his paper bag? Why does he urgently want to see the manager?

I know I can count on you not to tell us (a) he's got a gun in the bag and he's going to rob the store or (b) he's got his lunch in the bag, he's hot and tired, taking his noon break and wants an air-conditioned, quiet place to eat his meal or (c) the manager is his fiancée, he's got an engagement ring in the bag, and this is his novel way to propose to her. None of the above, please.

AVOID THE OBVIOUS.

The ball is in your court. Go to work.

In my writing I tell the story of my life, over and over again.
—Isaac Bashevis Singer

. . . historically, anyone who gets away from "the story's the thing" loses money, period.
—Joe Roth, Disney Studio Chairman, quoted in *Time magazine*

Even after you've won fame and fortune, every time you write, you've got to write, there's no short cut, you have to start your career all over again.
—William Saroyan, *Sons Come and Go, Mothers Hang in Forever*

New Big Talent on the Block

An Interview with

Frank Darabont

"I put the effort into the job and I wound up with a hun-dred-and-some-odd pages, and it was absolutely dreadful. But you go again. And then you go on to the next one. You just devote the time to do it. Like practicing a musical instrument, you get better at it. But talent is like a brick wall. You're in a very tight space, and you're taking a run at that wall every time you sit down to write. Crashing into the wall is the equivalent of finding the limit of your abilities—it's very painful, but every time you do it, you push the wall back a little more."

—Frank Darabont

With the release of *Shawshank Redemption* in 1994, screenwriter-director Frank Darabont became an "overnight" Hollywood superstar as both a screenwriter and a film director. Like most "overnight" stars, Darabont's success was nine years in the making, which is just about par for the course in the tough, highly competitive movie industry.

It must have been especially affirming to this very gifted young man following the humiliating critical and audience response to *Mary Shelley's Frankenstein*, for which he received co-screenplay credit. That disaster was apparently the all-too-frequent result of the director and the screenwriter having different visions of what they were trying to put on the screen. As everybody in the industry knows, when that happens, the screenwriter might as well pack up and move to another planet; he is suddenly an unwanted non-entity. (When my first television script went into production, I was advised by the producer that the director routinely barred writers from the set!)

Young Frank Darabont, the French-born son of Hungarian refugees, was brought to America when he was an infant. His is a very American story. He started near the bottom of the filmmaker's ladder (working first as a production assistant, then in set construction and as a set decorator), learning everything he could about the making of movies. His goal was to become a screenwriter and he pursued it in his off hours with a relentless determination. Talent with an equal portion of tenacity are the key ingredients for any young filmmaker determined to make it to the top rung of the ladder. It's the Horatio Alger story for the '90s, as American as Mom's microwave.

By 1983, he had written and directed a thirty-minute film based on a short story by Stephen King. King must have liked what he saw; he enthusiastically supported Frank's decision to leap into the big time with his feature-film version of King's story *Shawshank Redemption*. The film was nominated for seven Academy Awards, including Best Picture and Best Screenplay. Frank's script was also nominated for a Writers Guild Award, the Golden Globe Award, and won the USC Scripter Award, the Pen Center USA West Award, the Humanitas Prize, and the Crystal Heart Award. Frank was also nominated as Best Director by the Directors Guild of America.

It would be hard to imagine a screenwriter and/or a feature-film director making a more impressive debut. And, as you will discover in the following pages, Frank Darabont is a very impressive young man.

FROUG: What is the toughest assignment you've had as a screenwriter?

DARABONT: Golly, I don't remember. Each one has its challenges that are unique to that particular assignment.

FROUG: In *Shawshank Redemption*, you took a very slim story and made it into a two-hour-plus movie that was, to many people, the best movie of the year, and deserved the Oscar. What did you see in this story that turned you on to it?

DARABONT: Well, it doesn't run on too many pages. But within those pages was an incredibly rich story that spanned a lot of years. It seemed to me that the elements that story contained were just crying out to be made into a film. Frankly, I'm grateful the story wasn't any longer, because I had trouble containing the movie to a two-hour-and-twenty-minute film.

FROUG: What did you see in the story that would hold dramatic tension?

DARABONT: My instantaneous reaction, my visceral reaction, was to be incredibly uplifted by the ending that Stephen King wrote. I found myself quite moved; it really brought tears when I first read it. In terms of dramatic tension throughout, I loved the journey that these characters go on. In the case of Andy, here was a man coming to terms with his environment, with the evil in other people, with the hopelessness of that place, and yet existing on hope. I found that fascinating. And as far as Red is concerned, it was the echo effect that Andy's journey has on him, his wrestling between hope and despair and choosing hope. That was the whole thematic spine of the story.

FROUG: Choosing hope?

DARABONT: I found it totally compelling.

FROUG: It makes the whole picture come together. Did you start with that concept of the theme somewhere in your mind?

DARABONT: Absolutely. The theme was so present in King's story that I took my cue from there. That's really what I latched onto when I first read it. It took me on the journey with those characters, and examined the nature of hope and the nature of human dignity. And it did it in a very entertaining way, which makes it sort of a pop storytelling device. It's within the context of an entertaining yarn that a very classic and meaningful story is told.

FROUG: Yes it is. Did you always have Morgan Freeman in mind?

DARABONT: Well, Morgan was a suggestion made by Liz Glotzer at Castle Rock, who was our executive on the show. Morgan had not been in my mind, because the character was written by Stephen King as a white Irishman. So the suggestion of Morgan came as a bit of a surprise, but it only took a few minutes for my producer and me to turn it over in our heads and realize that it was an absolutely brilliant suggestion. He embodied that character.

FROUG: I think it was the best performance he's ever given.

DARABONT: It was just amazing. He brought dignity and wisdom to that character in a way that I don't know any other actor could have done.

FROUG: Coming off of that super success, are you now swamped with people sending you screenplays to adapt or to rewrite or to direct?

DARABONT: All of the above.

FROUG: Is it fun?

DARABONT: You know, everything brings its own set of problems along with it. But these are all good problems to have. At the moment, I'm feeling a little worn out and wishing that I hadn't taken on quite so much this year. This has turned out to be a fairly heavy writing year for me. I've done some rewrites for some other folks, and I have yet to write the two screenplays for Castle Rock that I'm attached to direct.

FROUG: So you have a commitment with Castle Rock for two more films?

DARABONT: Yes.

FROUG: Well, they're smart.

DARABONT: They're also by far the best place in town to make a movie, I think.

FROUG: Do you prefer directing or writing?

DARABONT: Well, it depends on what I'm doing at the time. If I'm directing, I certainly prefer writing. [Laughter] When you're writing and you're isolated and you're locked away in the house, you start thinking, "Gee, it'd be nice to be on a set again." The grass is always greener, as you know. I think that if I had to answer that question honestly, I'd say writing. I find directing very, very difficult.

FROUG: You're talking eleven- or twelve-hour days, right?

DARABONT: Try twelve- to sixteen-hour days for the director.

FROUG: On your feet all that time?

DARABONT: On your feet, or even if you're not on your feet, your brain is on its feet. You're always doing your homework for the following day, or agonizing over what didn't go right *that* day and how to compensate for it. The vagaries of filmmaking will buffet you as you go along, and you have to be thinking on your feet quite a lot. When you get that worn out, physically and mentally, it's very difficult to keep going. It's not a fun occupation. But I've never believed that the worth of any human endeavor should be measured by how much fun it is. I don't think things are achieved that way. I'm sure Edison didn't invent the light bulb because it was fun to do. He did it for other reasons.

FROUG: As the director of *Shawshank*, did you ever get mad at the screenwriter—you?

"I've never believed that the worth of any human endeavor should be measured by how much fun it is."

[32]

DARABONT: Oh, not mad, exactly. But fed up from time to time. Like, "Oh, my God, why did this guy write it this way?"

FROUG: It's not simple to wear both hats at the same time?

DARABONT: Simple, no. But, actually, it's a great pleasure. I found great pleasure in directing my own material. I've had a few good experiences as a screenwriter, seeing another director take my material and put it on the screen. But not often. Most of them seemed lacking.

FROUG: Well, one of them that might have been lacking, at least according to the critics and the audience, was *Mary Shelley's Frankenstein*.

DARABONT: I'd have to agree with the critics and the audience on that one. I was not happy with the way the movie turned out.

FROUG: How could the guy who did *Shawshank Redemption* have done this movie?

DARABONT: The guy who did *Shawshank Redemption* didn't do that movie.

FROUG: Tell me about that.

DARABONT: Kenneth Branagh directed *Frankenstein*. I have to swallow my disappointment and chalk it up to the age-old difference between what the screenwriter intended and what the director made. Clearly Ken and I had two different movies in mind.

FROUG: For the director, what the writer wants is secondary. Right?

DARABONT: It is. Because film, ultimately, for better or for worse, is the director's medium. He or she is the one with the final say, the one who has to walk onto the set every morning and do the job with conviction. Oftentimes, that results in wonderful things. At other times, it results in less optimal things.

FROUG: Who was Steph Lady, the first screenwriter credited on *Mary Shelley's Frankenstein*?

DARABONT: Steph is the writer who wrote the original draft of *Frankenstein*, which I was then hired to rewrite.

FROUG: Branagh hired you to rewrite it?

DARABONT: Actually, the studio hired me to rewrite it with Branagh's blessing.

FROUG: Did you meet with him?

DARABONT: Yes, I did. I had a week of story meetings with Ken in London prior to writing. Then I flew back and wrote the script in six weeks flat, writing around the clock. It was a very tough schedule. It was a very big job.

FROUG: I have to assume that you got into a major rewrite because the Writers Guild gives you co-screenplay credit, and we both know the Guild credit system leans heavily toward the first writer. It's rare that the second writer ends up sharing equal credit. In this case, it is a Steph Lady and Frank Darabont credit, which means that you had to change the story and the characters substantially.

DARABONT: This is not to put Steph down at all, but I felt that his draft had drifted too far from Mary Shelley's story. For me, the challenge and the pleasure of writing that script was to sort of lasso it and pull it back into Mary Shelley's world. It was more an issue of sitting down and adapting the book, while retaining Steph's material that really worked, some terrific ideas. I certainly didn't want to throw him out completely. That serves nobody's interest. I was really very proud of my *Frankenstein* script. If one were to ask me for examples of my best work as a screenwriter, I'd say *Shawshank* and *Frankenstein*. But the resulting movies show you the difference between one director doing it and another.

FROUG: Yes, they do. Let me ask you about *Young Indiana Jones*, which was, to me, one of the most underrated TV series. You wrote seven or eight of those?

DARABONT: Yes. It was a lovely show.

FROUG: Was it canceled because the budget was too high?

DARABONT: No. This is a fallacy that was reinforced by the network, who wanted to pass it off to the public as special by virtue of having a big budget. They figured that if they touted the highest budget ever, it would have people's attention. The truth is, the show was budgeted at a million-and-a-half dollars per episode.

FROUG: Which, in today's world, is not that outrageous.

DARABONT: In fact, it's really right in line. The actual average cost for an hour TV show is nowadays around a million-and-a-half dollars per episode, maybe more. An episode of *Young Indiana Jones* was less expensive to produce than an average episode of *Murder, She Wrote*.

FROUG: Amazing.

DARABONT: What's more amazing are the *Young Indiana Jones* production values—what they were able to put on the screen for that cost.

FROUG: Every episode looked like a feature.

DARABONT: Absolutely. Great credit has to be given to the producer of that show, Rick McCallum, who was like General Patton with his troops, traveling the world shooting the shows. They shot in Africa. They shot all over Europe. They shot in the United States.

They shot damn near anywhere you can think of, and they did an amazing job. I think they were working for two solid years with very little time off. The attrition rate among the crew was very high because people burned out. But Rick McCallum never wore out, which said something about him as the producer. He was absolutely tireless.

FROUG: Well, George Lucas certainly did a courageous thing when he spent that much money to shoot the pilot and take a chance on getting a series out of it. How many of them were actually done?

DARABONT: Golly, we had two seasons' worth. What would that be? Over thirty episodes. But here's George doing amazing stuff, and ABC pulls the plug on it. I don't think ABC really understood the show, so I don't think they gave it much of a chance with the public.

FROUG: They didn't publicize it very much, except, as you say, its high budget.

DARABONT: And they kept bouncing the time slot around, which never helps. Instead of putting it early in the evening, when the kids would have been able to watch it as well, they always managed to put it late enough that the kids were already in bed. That left it with only the adults watching, and they weren't quite enough to put it over in the ratings.

FROUG: It's very rare for one writer to write seven or eight episodes of an hour series. That's an enormous amount of writing.

DARABONT: It was a lot of work. There were seven writers involved in the show. And we all wrote roughly seven episodes. It was a wonderful, marvelous experience.

FROUG: Was it a good training ground for features?

DARABONT: Absolutely. For me, particularly. It allowed me to stretch as a writer. It allowed me to write the kind of material that I wasn't often writing in Hollywood features, which is to say more character-oriented, character-driven stories. It allowed me to become more comfortable with that form in a way that I think benefited *Shawshank*.

FROUG: Eight one-hour scripts in a period of about a year and a half is the equivalent of four features.

DARABONT: Since then, George has combined, paired off, some remaining episodes that had yet to be shot when ABC pulled the plug and done them as *Young Indie* TV movies for the Family Channel. So there have been four two-hour *Young Indie* TV movies produced for cable. He hasn't let it go. He's a great believer in the show. It's just a shame that what we were trying was maybe a little too ambitious for the network to get behind or understand.

FROUG: It was surprisingly adult, I thought. The story and the characters were developed on the level of his features.

DARABONT: It was a very thoughtful approach.

FROUG: Knowing that screenwriters are the serfs of the industry or the peons of the industry, if you will, what in the world determined you to become a screenwriter?

DARABONT: The deep psychotic desire to be a storyteller, which was fostered at a very early age.

FROUG: Tell me about that.

DARABONT: I was always reading books and comic books, and I was always in love with storytelling in whatever form it took. And I always had a special leaning toward films. I remember when I

"I was always reading books and comic books, and I was always in love with storytelling in whatever form it took."

was five, my brother Andy took me to my first movie in a real theater. It was this charming, cheesy, science-fiction movie called *Robinson Crusoe on Mars*. It was one of those experiences, very early in life, that just sort of set you on the path.

FROUG: You were enchanted.

DARABONT: Enchanted, exactly. And, growing up with films, that enchantment was reinforced many times. They would just transport me to a different world. Things like *Planet of the Apes*, or *THX 1138*, which was George Lucas's very first film.

FROUG: I saw it at USC when he was first showing it as his student film.

DARABONT: A brilliant film and, unfortunately, underrated. There were also films like *The Bridge on the River Kwai* and Stanley Kubrick's body of work—those made a big impact. Absolute masterpieces. All those had an effect, as did many of Spielberg's films. I was fifteen when I saw *Jaws*. God, I was just completely transported. I wanted to be part of that storytelling.

FROUG: Did you take courses or did you read books on screenwriting? How did you make that transition from wanting to be to becoming?

DARABONT: For me, it was a process of doing. Throughout my life, I would write things. Even as a kid. After graduating from high school, I tried my hand at writing a feature screenplay, which is still sitting in a file cabinet somewhere and will never see the light of day. But I sat down and did it. I put the effort into the job and I wound up with hundred-and-some-odd pages, and it was absolutely dreadful. But you go again. And then you go on to the next one. You devote the time to do it. Like practicing a musical instrument, you get better at it. Talent is like a brick wall. You're in a very tight space, and you're taking a run at that wall every time you sit down to write. Crashing into the wall is the equivalent of finding the limit of your abilities—it's painful, but every time you do it, you push the wall back a little more. I'm always somewhat astounded when people who've never written sit down to write a screenplay with the intention of selling it, as if *selling* were the major concern. "Oh," they say, "I have to *sell* a screenplay." No, you have to learn how to *write* one first. Selling it will take care of itself later on, assuming you invest the time necessary to develop your skills. For me, it was a matter of years of trying to develop my writing in the same way that some people spend years learning to play the violin—they get better every time they play the scales. I was also helped along during that time by my bread-and-butter jobs in film production. I worked as a set dresser in the art department for six years. Purely free-lance, non-union stuff. I was barely making a living, but it was enough. I would get on a show, some low-budget film, and work for six weeks, maybe two months. That would put enough money in the bank to buy myself a month of time at home to write. When the bank account bottomed out, I'd go back and get another set dressing job.

FROUG: Meanwhile learning about shooting film.

DARABONT: Meanwhile learning the processes of making films. The position of set dresser is the best film school in the world.

FROUG: Because you're right there with the director all day.

DARABONT: Absolutely. You're with the actors and the cameraman. You're right in the eye of the storm, absorbing the process through your skin by observation and participation. So I was

"I'm always somewhat astounded when people who've never written sit down to write a screenplay with the intention of selling it, as if selling were the major concern."

learning that end of things with my "day job," and I was learning to write on my own by using that money to buy myself time. It was a struggle.

FROUG: My average UCLA student who's been successful wrote at least six complete, polished screenplays before finally selling one. It's just a process of writing and writing and writing.

DARABONT: And getting better and better and better. And it may take more than six scripts. It's like building a "talent bank account." You keep making small deposits in order to finally be able to make a large withdrawal some day. In my case, it took nine years after graduating from high school—I graduated in 1977, and it was not until 1986 that I started making a living as a writer. Those nine years involved a lot of struggle, a lot of effort. I feel very fortunate. It takes a lot of people even longer.

FROUG: The *Nightmare on Elm Street* series, you did the '87 version?

DARABONT: Yes, the third one. *Nightmare on Elm Street 3, Dream Warriors.* I wrote that script with Chuck Russell, a very old pal who is directing now. He hired me on my very first movie job as a production assistant. It was a movie called *Hell Night*, back in 1980. He was the production manager or line producer, I forget exactly. That was back in *his* struggling years. We discovered that we shared a desire to write, so we started writing together around then. We turned out a lot of scripts until, finally, in 1986 he was hired to come in and fix the script of *Nightmare on Elm Street 3*, and direct the film. So he enlisted me and we wrote that script together in eleven days, working around the clock. Maybe two weeks after finishing the script, Chuck was on the set directing it.

FROUG: Baptism by fire is the worst. But it's a hell of a learning process.

DARABONT: Oh, yeah. The pressure's on, you've got to get it done.

FROUG: And after that, you went on to *The Blob*. How was that experience?

DARABONT: Very pleasant. I've always enjoyed working with Chuck. He's a very dear friend, and we have a wonderful time together. And I think he's a damn good writer, too. Funny enough, among all the features I've written—with the exception of *Shawshank*, with which I am most satisfied—I think that the two films I'm probably happiest with, in the way they turned out, would be *Nightmare 3* and *The Blob*.

FROUG: In both cases, the director followed the screenwriter and the screenplay.

DARABONT: We had the advantages of the director *being* one of the screenwriters. Of course, he would follow the script. I don't know why other directors feel compelled to change things as they go along.

FROUG: Is it ego? Is it just being obstinate? What's the story on that? Sometimes the director can make movies critically better, of course.

DARABONT: Of course. That's what directors are trying for, to improve the film as they see it. I guess we just answered our own question.

FROUG: But more often than not they don't. I've found that it's rare for a director to have respect for a screenwriter's work.

DARABONT: Well, this is not to say that every screenplay is a work of gold. I think a lot of scripts are improvable, and a lot are flat-out terrible and need work. So I'm not clothing writers here in a mantle of sanctity, anything but. It's just that the door swings both ways—sometimes the writer has done a *terrific* job, and the people

"I do find a lot
of directors
seem frightened
of the words."

making the film can't recognize it. I do find a lot of directors seem frightened of the *words*.

FROUG: Sometimes I have discovered that they actually haven't studied the script. I know of several specific cases on big-budget movies.

DARABONT: From my perspective, sometimes they really haven't read the script carefully enough. And they do seem to have a terrible fear of words, as I said. My greatest complaint about the work I've had produced is that the *words* I put down on the page—which I try to make as interesting and as sophisticated as I can—are the first things to suffer. They'll take pages of dialogue and find a way to simplify things, to homogenize the components. They'll simplify to the point of becoming dumb. That's what's disheartening. This is why I think Quentin Tarantino is so good—he's not afraid of words. He rambles around in his words, he rolls around in his words, and he's incredibly good at writing those words.

FROUG: Well, there again is a case of a man directing his own screenplays. It seems to make a huge difference.

DARABONT: It seems to be a fairly good argument for a good writer directing his or her own work.

FROUG: Going back to previous generations, Billy Wilder is a pretty good case in point.

DARABONT: Absolutely. Directing one's own screenplay seems to help retain an overall vision that, in my experience, otherwise might not exist. In all fairness, though, there are countless examples of movies that have turned out wonderfully the other way, where a director *enhances* the script he was given.

FROUG: Do you know offhand of any films where the director made drastic changes in the screenplay *and* made the picture much better? I'm not saying that they don't exist, but I'm hard pressed to think of one.

DARABONT: Well, there are times when the directors don't make drastic changes. They take what's there and optimize, maximize the screenplay. You'd have to ask Eric Roth about this, but I don't imagine that the *Forrest Gump* script was messed with drastically—perhaps just intelligently refined.

FROUG: Eric was thrilled and delighted. He worked very closely with Zemeckis, and they did follow the script. Another great example is Dave Peoples' *Unforgiven*. Clint Eastwood loved the screenplay and made only the most minor revisions, consulting with Dave on anything he thought about changing.

DARABONT: I guess the classic example of a movie script changing right and left, yet still resulting in one of the best movies ever, was *Casablanca*.

FROUG: Yes, but that's a rare case.

DARABONT: Sometimes lightening does strike that way. But more often than not, I think we have to start out with the screenplay, nurture it and take care of it, instead of thinking of it as the enemy. I can't imagine going into production on a film without having the script locked down, which is not to say that things don't change anyway in reasonable creative collaboration with your actors, writer, cinematographer, whomever. Anybody working on a film can have worthwhile creative ideas, and you have to listen to those ideas. It *is*, ultimately, a collaborative effort.

FROUG: Absolutely.

DARABONT: But, you should also consider the overall context and the overall vision. What was the original intention? In *Shawshank,* I tried to keep it to the original concept. You don't want to turn it into something else. Lord knows, there are a million reasons things change while making a film. You know, the weather goes bad, the set falls down, the actor has health problems—but whatever happens, you always try to hammer it back into shape and get it back on track. You're going toward a destination. You've got to remember your overall vision.

FROUG: The writer has the same problem, right? When you're writing, you have to constantly remind yourself to keep it on track.

DARABONT: Yes. Then, during shooting, you have a lot of people not necessarily challenging you, but certainly questioning you. They come in with their own ideas, some of which are quite valuable and not to be ignored. But the screenplay is the foundation you're working from.

FROUG: We're trying to get to a point where there's a little more respect for the writer. Do you think there is hope through the Writers Guild and the Directors Guild reaching some sort of agreement?

DARABONT: No. You can't legislate for respect. Respect comes from a working collaboration among people who are willing to respect each other. That's something you cannot mandate. Some directors will always view the writer as the enemy. Other directors, the smart ones, realize that the collaboration between the writer and the director is one of the most significant creative collaborations that we have in filmmaking, at least as significant

"You can't legislate for respect. Respect comes from a working collaboration among people who are willing to respect each other."

as the collaboration with actors. Those directors are the ones I respect the most: the Steven Spielbergs, the Dick Donners. Dick is a wonderful man and, in my experience, an example of how a director works in collaboration with a writer.

FROUG: For many years, he was my closest personal friend.

DARABONT: I love Dick. He's one of the most gracious and loving men. Of all the directors I've worked with or observed, either as a writer or as a set dresser, I'd say that Dick is one of the most generous. In my experience, the most secure directors seem to be the most inclusive of others—not just the writer, but the actors, the crew, you name it. They keep a firm hand on the reins, but they also realize that they stand to gain a lot from the creative input of others. The *least* secure ones seem threatened by creative input. They try to control things in a fascistic way and are frightened by other people's ideas.

FROUG: How is the 500-channel information superhighway going to impact the marketplace for all the wannabe screenwriters?

DARABONT: I think it's going to expand the market. I think it's a very healthy thing, in the same way that the advent of the home video player was incredibly healthy to our business. It will just add more and more venues to bring the product to the consumer. It's an ever-expanding pie, if you will. The bigger the pie, the more opportunities there are, the more work there is. In other words, the more opportunities we have for a film to be successful, the better off we are. Twenty years ago, if a film wasn't making any money in its initial theatrical release, it was a failure. Now a film not only has the theatrical release, it has video, pay-for-view, cable—it has all these various venues that all generate income.

FROUG: Those things that used to be called ancillary markets are becoming primary markets.

DARABONT: They are becoming primary markets. *Shawshank*, for example, didn't do all that well in its initial run—well, it actually did okay, thanks to the Oscar nominations. People finally went to the theater to see it, which was great. Nevertheless, we're going to make most of our money from the so-called ancillary markets, like video. We're one of the most-rented tapes this year.

FROUG: I'm not surprised. I hope you have a piece of this action?

DARABONT: Oh, sure. I'm a member of both of the Writers Guild and the Directors Guild, and they have residual formulas. Every time a tape is bought, they'll go chunk-a-chink with some money for us. In a month or two, we're going to have our sell-through release on videocassette. In other words, it will no longer be "priced for rental," ninety dollars, it will be priced for sale at less than twenty dollars. The consumer will be able to walk in and buy it and take it home, and that's another great influx of capital in recouping the cost of a film.

FROUG: Frank, is there any comment you want to make before we close?

DARABONT: Well, here's something for those people who want to get in this field and become screenwriters: I know the goal seems quite far out of reach, but I think I'm proof that all things are possible. I wasn't born into this business. I wasn't even born in this country. My parents brought me over when I was a baby. My earliest memories are of living in a Chicago tenement on the immigrant side of town. So I came to this business totally out of left field. Totally cold.

FROUG: You're living proof that, as you say, anything is possible.

DARABONT: Anything *is* possible. And that applies to all things in life, not just the movie business. It's just a matter of determination, passion, and the willingness to invest effort. I think the sky's the limit, but that doesn't mean it's easy. Anybody who thinks it's easy is only fooling themselves. John F. Kennedy said it best: "We choose to go to the moon, not because it is easy, but because it is hard." If you live by that, you can go to the moon!

CREDITS

Nightmare on Elm Street 3: Dream Warriors (shared writing credit)

The Blob (shared writing credit)

The Fly II (shared writing credit)

Buried Alive (director)

Mary Shelley's Frankenstein (shared writing credit)

The Young Indiana Jones Chronicles (writer: seven episodes)

Tales from the Crypt (writer: two episodes)

    1990 Writers Guild nomination for "The Ventriloquist's Dummy" episode.

Shawshank Redemption (writer-director)

    Academy Award nomination for Best Picture and Best Screenplay

    Writers Guild of America nomination for Best Adapted Screenplay

    Golden Globe nomination for Best Screenplay

    Directors Guild of America nomination for Best Director

    USC Scripter Award for Best Book to Film Adaptation

    Pen Center USA West Award for Best Screenplay

    Humanitas Prize for Best Screenplay

    Crystal Heart Award for Feature Film

A Heart as Big as the Ritz

An Interview with

Bo Goldman

". . . when writing a screenplay, you have to imagine
everything that's on the screen . . . what's between the
words, between the sentences. The mortar, so to speak.
You have to have a vision as a screenwriter. You're not
writing, you're envisioning something. And then that
vision ultimately, if everything works out perfectly,
becomes realized. The closest I ever came to it was in
Scent of a Woman. I felt that the director took whatever
vision I had, distilled it, and took it further. And that's the
dream you have as a screenwriter."

—Bo Goldman

The unique signature of every Bo Goldman film is an empathy for characters—a warmth and depth of understanding and caring—that few other screenwriters can bring to their work. To see a Bo Goldman movie is to experience the feelings of his characters.

What's his secret? It's the oldest "secret" in the world. If you want to really touch people's hearts, you first have to touch your own. But do it, as Bo does, without cheap or easy sentimentality. Sentimentality is a one-minute fix, cotton candy. Bo's work is spun gold, a wealth of human emotions. You remember his characters long after the movie is over.

I believe that whenever Bo writes a screenplay, he goes deeply inside himself, where he discovers not only his own feelings but the universal feelings of us all. And do we respond to it? Bet on it. Bo's screenplays have a habit of winning Oscars, Writers Guild Awards, plus many nominations. They become classics no matter who directs them. He is one of the most sought-after screenwriters in Hollywood yet, by his choice, he is little known personally. A shy, introspective man, he lives in a tiny town in the northern tip of California, coming to Hollywood only when work demands his presence.

I've known and admired Bo for many years, and I am honored and delighted to introduce him to you now.

FROUG: How did you get started as a screenwriter?

GOLDMAN: Necessity. I had six children. I was an aspiring librettist in the musical theater. I always wanted to be Oscar Hammerstein and I never got there. Way back in 1959, I had a musical on Broadway called "First Impressions," which was based on *Pride and Prejudice*. That was my first show. The cast included Hermione Gingold, Farley Granger, and Polly Bergen. Abe Burrows directed it.

FROUG: That's a pretty big cast.

GOLDMAN: I remember that Brooks Atkinson, who was head critic for the *New York Times*, said Farley Granger played Darcy with all the flexibility of a telephone pole.

FROUG: [Laughter] That was a wonderful way to start your career, right?

GOLDMAN: It was quite a wonderful thing, but it was a flop. But not quite a flop. Jule Styne had high regards for me—I was kind of a protégé of his. Jule said, "I've had flops of every dimension and, Bo, this is not a flop." He was a wonderful man; I loved him.

"First Impressions" ran about three months. Then I was ten years trying to get my second one on Broadway. It was a Civil War story that I began at the start of the Centennial. We went through a string of directors. Arthur Penn was the director for a while. There was a bunch in between, and we ended up with Jerome Robbins. But somehow it just didn't happen.

I was young and had a large family. And you know the old story about Broadway: You can't make a living, you can only make a killing. I was starving, and when my parents died around the recession of 1970, '71, and '72, I kind of bottomed out. I had to farm my children out. They worked as au pairs for my rich friends and contacts I'd made during my years at Princeton, who by now were either the head of pediatrics somewhere or partners in White and Case or Smith, Barney. It was humiliating. It was horrible. But I kept working. I did a Christmas show for PBS called *An American Christmas: Words and Music*. Ed Sherin, Jane Alexander's husband, directed it. I produced and wrote it—wrote the songs for it and everything. It was one of the hardest things in the world to do a Christmas show, but it was a huge success. At the same time, this friend and I were talking about all the marriages that were breaking up around me, including my brother's, but not my own, and I had a thought for a movie. Well, this ultimately became *Shoot the Moon*.

FROUG: Which I love. I think it's a classic.

GOLDMAN: Although it was not commercially successful, it does have a following. I read a very learned book written by the head of a film department, I think it was at Holy Cross, who said it was the best movie of the '80s. He saw some things in it that I didn't know were there. He said it told the truth about marriage. But this script sure kicked around for a while.

FROUG: For how long?

GOLDMAN: Nine years before it was done. An agent, Robby Lantz, read *Shoot the Moon* as a favor to my brother, a real-estate magnate from Bermuda who died broke. *Shoot the Moon* was my entry. Robby said, "I think you can make a living doing this." He gave the script to Stuart Millar, a producer of some repute. He did *Little Big Man*, which Arthur Penn directed. Anyway, Stuart was trying to become a director. He had directed something called *When The Legends Die*, but he couldn't get his next movie going. And then other people began to see my *Shoot the Moon*. The script became what they call a "calling card." I hate that expression. I used to ask why would I want a calling card? Then Peter Bart, a former studio executive at Paramount, was trying to get a writer. He'd become an independent producer, partnered with a rich guy named Max Palevsky, and they had bought Dan Wakefield's book *Starting Over*. So my first job was working on that screenplay. And five years later, it became a movie written by Jim Brooks.

Meanwhile, Milos Forman heard of my work. Jack Nicholson was getting rubbery about doing *One Flew Over the Cuckoo's Nest*. They had a script that wasn't going to work, and they wanted someone to come in on it. Milos, who had read the script of *Shoot the Moon*, came to see me. He asked me what I would do with *Cuckoo's Nest*. I had a few ideas. One was when McMurphy arrives, he should kiss one of the guards. Milos said, "Oh, I like that." And he hired me. Years later, Milos said that the kiss was what interested him in me right away—how I thought about the movie, you know. Strange, isn't it? That was the first script that I really worked on with a director. And it was the first movie I had produced.

FROUG: And you won an Oscar for *Cuckoo's Nest*, which was magnificent. I remember you told me once that Milos Forman said to you, "Forget the book. This is a movie, it's an entirely different thing."

"A movie is not a director's movie or a star's movie or anybody's movie."

GOLDMAN: Well, we talked about adaptation, about how you have to declare war on the original property and still respect it and remember from whence it comes. But after that, you mustn't let yourself be trapped by it.

FROUG: By trying to be too faithful to what was basically a narrative story as opposed to drama?

GOLDMAN: Yeah. Everything has to be reconceived, even when you write an original movie. A movie is not a director's movie or a star's movie or anybody's movie. Once the movie gets shot, it becomes its own thing. It's its own organism. It's during post-production, with music added and so on, that the baby is really being born. It's the only period when you cannot force anything new out of it. You can't make it shorter. You can't make it longer. You can't cut somebody out to make some star look better. You can't cut to the chase. It will be what it wants to be. And if you fool with what it wants to be, you'll kill it.

FROUG: For the moment, let's not get too carried away from the screenplay, which is the basic root of the whole movie.

GOLDMAN: What I say all the time is that the screenplay is the blood of the movie. It's what gives the movie life. But what you see on the page is not necessarily what the movie is, even though every word you write may be shot. For instance, in my first adaptation, *American Christmas: Words and Music*, from a story by Grace Paley called "The Loudest Voice," I would use some of her dialogue verbatim, but it just wouldn't play. Although everybody loved that short film, I learned a lot from that experience. I learned that, when writing a screenplay, you have to imagine everything that's on screen . . . what's between the words, between the sentences. The mortar, so to speak. You have to have a vision as a screenwriter. You're not writing, you're envisioning something. And then that vision ultimately, if everything works perfectly, becomes realized. The closest I ever came to that ideal was in *Scent of a Woman*. I felt that the director took whatever vision I had, distilled it, and took it further. He saw his job just like a director does in the theater. He interpreted the author's ideas. And that's the dream you have as a screenwriter.

FROUG: You got an Oscar nomination for that one, too.

GOLDMAN: I did. And I was very happy for the movie's recognition. I know that you've been the most wonderful defender and proponent of screenwriting, but I think it's still an emerging art. I never saw a lawyer in my life until I started to make some money, and then I got one lawsuit after another. [Laughter] And I remember one of these lawyers, representing somebody who's coming out of the woodwork claiming I'd just stolen their life, said something about my "craft." Well, you know, it's not a craft. Whenever I hear the word craft, I think of a rainy day at Camp Wigwam, where you throw darts and make leather pouches. It's not a craft, it's an art. It takes the sensibility of an artist. And a lot of great writers who are novelists or journalists can't do it. It's something you have to learn. I remember once when I was talking to the wife of one of those fancy folk I went to school with, she asked me to help a novelist who has since received the MacArthur Foundation thing, that $250,000 life grant or whatever. She said, "Oh, we're trying to get him work because he's having hard times. He's one of us, can

"Whenever I hear the word craft, I think of a rainy day at Camp Wigwam, where you throw darts and make leather pouches."

you get him a screenplay?" [Laughter] Sort of like it was some kind of slumming.

FROUG: Like taking in laundry?

GOLDMAN: Yeah, or a courtesan starting to hit the streets. A phrase that I cannot abide is "Hollywood screenwriter." Why am I a Hollywood screenwriter? In how many countless sports stories or news stories do they say, "No Hollywood screenwriter could have invented this." It's like saying "Beverly Hills doctor." There are many wonderful doctors in Beverly Hills, but one thinks of a Beverly Hills doctor as someone who does plastic surgery.

FROUG: You had a bitter experience with your credit on *City Hall.*

GOLDMAN: It's hard to go into the details of it because it's unseemly.

FROUG: This is an original of yours?

GOLDMAN: It's not an original of mine. I'm one of four writers— one team and two others—on this screenplay. The man who originated it, a former deputy mayor of New York, was an extremely wealthy investment banker. He had the germ of an idea, which was taken to Paul Schrader to direct. And then Schrader, who's also a writer, brought in other writers and on and on . . .

[Interviewer's Note: Bo and I proceeded into a lengthy discussion of the present Writers Guild of America's controversial credit-arbitration system, which has recently been voted upon because of the complaints of many screenwriters. Eighty percent of the membership voted against changing the present system.]

FROUG: The Writers Guild is in the process of voting on revising those rules, to get away from the overwhelming bias toward the first writer.

GOLDMAN: It is overwhelming. Anyway, what I worry about is the nature of those who follow this profession. I want to be proud to be called a screenwriter. There you are, Bill, devoting your emeritus years to getting us credit for what we do, and yet there's this kind of odd, cynical, and bitter quality in many of us, too many of us. I remember being appalled at the first Writers Guild Awards dinner I went to. I wondered why are these people so angry? What are they so angry about?

I remember, in the mid-'70s, going to those screenings at the Writers Guild Theater, and the hooting and booing that was going on. I thought, well, one of us wrote this movie, didn't we? Why would we want to do this to each other? It could be the worst movie, but who knows how it started out? Who knows how it could have been corrupted? What they can do to your work is terrible. And, ultimately, they throw back at you this "Hollywood screenwriter" thing: What are you bitching about? Look at your paycheck. Well, that's never an answer.

FROUG: *Melvin and Howard*, to me, was a classic. How'd you wind up creating a marvelous story about Howard Hughes and the guy who picked him up?

GOLDMAN: Well, it was interesting. I met Ned Tanen, the head of Universal, who's been a friend for years and somebody I dearly love, when I wrote what they called a "shadow" *King Kong*. I was such a novice. They had me and the director, Joe

" . . . what I worry about is the nature of those who follow this profession. I want to be proud to be called a screenwriter."

Sargent, doing a *King Kong* screenplay without telling us about another *King Kong* script of Dino DeLaurentis'.

FROUG: You were writing about a guy sitting on a park bench at the zoo, am I right?

GOLDMAN: That's right. You remember all that?

FROUG: Yeah. I was fascinated by your offbeat approach.

GOLDMAN: So that's how I met Ned. And then he called me one day and said that he had just bought this story of the guy who was one of the heirs to the Howard Hughes estate. Ned asked, "Are you interested?" I said, "No, I'm not interested in Howard Hughes." He said, "Will you do me a favor, go see this guy?" So the next day I went to Ogden, Utah. I went to the gas station behind which Melvin lived. I talked to this guy and he fascinated me. I guess I felt as if I were he, because of the years of struggling and having no money. I knew what it was like. Somehow he was some Mormon version of me, [Laughter] now struggling with no money and no everything. So I talked to him for a day or two and then went back to Universal and said, "I'll do it." Then I came back again to Utah and lived with Melvin for a month. We took the trip in which he found Hughes. We started from Gabbs, Nevada, and we ended up in Anaheim, California, where his ex-wife, Linda, was. Mary Steenburgen played her part in the movie, and won an Oscar for it, too.

FROUG: Did you believe his story?

GOLDMAN: Yes. Absolutely. I do. And I think the proof of it is that they never even charged him with any malfeasance. But he was the first one to tell me that he would never get any of the money. When I said goodbye to Melvin in Anaheim, he said, "What do you think? Do you think I'll ever see the money?" I said, "Well, *I* believe you." And he said, "I'll never see the money. What chance have I got against Howard Hughes' family and heirs?" And he was right. Then, some time later, process servers representing Howard Hughes' cousins' lawyers appeared at my door, trying to subpoena my material. So Universal said, "Get out of town now!" I went to Lake Tahoe and wrote the movie there. I came back with it and met with one of the producers, a guy named Art Linson, who's been around. He said that it was wonderful and that the character that I made really was Melvin. Then you know how the movie went. It wasn't a financial success, but it got a lot of recognition.

FROUG: If you had a percentage of the net, you'd never see a dime, anyway.

GOLDMAN: Yeah, right. It opened the New York Film Festival, which was a big success in New York. Melvin came out for it. We were in a box together, and I remember that we stood at the end. He raised his arm and everybody stood up and cheered. That was a great moment.

FROUG: Did he like it?

GOLDMAN: Oh, he liked it very much. And then, years later, I heard from him. He was selling frozen fish. He also had a lounge act briefly in Nevada, but was broke again. It was so sad.

FROUG: So do you think he basically was shafted by the overpowering presence of these Hughes attorneys and executives?

GOLDMAN: Well, yeah. What chance was Melvin going to have? What chance was the Mormon Church, which was part of the will, going to have? What chance were the Boy Scouts going to have? It was a business situation and he lost. We now know that justice is purchasable.

FROUG: Of all your films, which one is your favorite?

GOLDMAN: I think *Scent of a Woman*. It's my favorite only because I feel like I matured, and the movie reflects that. I don't want to put myself before the movie, because in the end you are always serving the movie. I hope that's clear. You're trying to create this child, this organism, this thing that everybody will want to go to and be diverted by. And you have to bring every element of your life to it. I mean, I'd gone to Exeter, which is a place it took me years to forget. I realized it was so antithetical . . .

FROUG: To a man who is essentially an artistic personality.

GOLDMAN: Yeah! All of the people there were being trained for the establishment. And I totally forget all of it. It was always way in the background. Years and years go by. I had been estranged from most of my family, and still am from the ones I grew up with and my long-lost brother, who made millions in mortgage brokerage, became an alcoholic, and had a terribly tragic life. Then I got this SOS from another brother of mine who said the once-rich brother was going to need a conservator. He was living in a big, expensive New York apartment, a year behind in his rent, and had no money at all. I went there and found him living in a kind of shabby elegance. The skeletons of his life were riddled with moral cancer, to strike a phrase.

"I don't want to put myself before the movie, because in the end you are always serving the movie. I hope that's clear. You're trying to create this child, this organism, this thing which everybody will want to go to and be diverted by."

A week later, I came back to California and got a call from Marty Brest, who showed me this sort of forgotten Italian movie, *Profuma di Donna*. I looked at this movie, and this character struck me as being exactly like my brother, who became the character in *Scent of a Woman*.

FROUG: I'll be damned.

GOLDMAN: The character was crossed with my first sergeant in the Army, a member of the famous 442nd Regimental Combat Team, who was the second man I've ever really been afraid of, and the first man I was afraid of—my father. The sergeant was a real soldier. He didn't do anything else except shine his shoes and live in a barracks. Once I saw him in Central Park in a rowboat, rowing a girl, and I thought this was his greatest diversion. So this character became a hybrid of all these people.

FROUG: I think the truth of your films, by and large, is that you always write from your gut feelings.

GOLDMAN: Yeah. I think that's also the joy. How do you feel about something? You're forced to find out within the structure of this art. You could go your whole life without finding out that stuff or what's tough and buried. I don't mean in your mind, but in your heart.

FROUG: And that's what comes on the screen with your work. It's, frankly, why I think of you as the Dean of American Screenwriters, and I'm certainly not alone in my opinion.

GOLDMAN: Thank you so much. Knowing you and your work, I'm really honored.

"How do you feel about something? You're forced to find out within the structure of this art."

FROUG: What your movies all have in common is heart. You know, your great Jewish heart.

GOLDMAN: Yes, it is! And after all those schools my father sent me to so that I wouldn't be Jewish. [Laughter]

CREDITS

City Hall, 1995 (shared credit)
Scent of a Woman, 1992 (original screenplay)
  (Oscar nominee)
Little Nikita, 1987
Shoot the Moon, 1981 (original story and screenplay)
Melvin and Howard, 1979 (original story and screenplay)
  (Oscar winner)
The Rose, 1979 (shared credit)
One Flew Over the Cuckoo's Nest, 1975 (shared credit)
  (Oscar winner)

There is no royal path to good writing; and such paths as do exist do not lead through neat critical gardens, various as they are, but through the jungles of self, the world, and of craft.
—Jessamyn West, *Saturday Review, 9/21/57*

When the characters are really alive before their author, the latter does nothing but follow them in their action, in their words, in the situations which they suggest to him.
—Luigi Pirandello, *Six Characters in Search of an Author*

Art, like life, should be free, since both are experimental.
—George Santayana, *The Life of Reason: Reason in Art*

Fake It Till You Make IT

Almost all screenwriters will tell you that the most difficult moment in their writing lives is when they face the blank page, especially page one. No mountain ever seems higher.

I once knew a highly successful screenwriter, one of the all-time greats, who spent a year writing and rewriting and rewriting page one. I know this first-hand because he asked me to come down to his office at 20th Century-Fox one day to proudly show me his new screenplay. (I was under contract to Fox for two years, writing and producing a one-hour drama series, *Adventures in Paradise*.)

"What do you think of it?" he said, smiling proudly as he leaned back in his chair.

He handed me only one page, perfectly typed, marked page one. I read it and handed it back to him. "Jim," I told him, "this is the same page you gave me to read a year ago, isn't it?"

"Sure," he said, "but this time I know I've got it right."

The fear of page one dogs us all. No matter how many years we practice our art, this fear never leaves us. But there are ways around it, especially when you are a beginner, before you've put a mountain of pressure on yourself to hit a home run.

Here's an exercise that will help you get started:

First, title your cover sheet—name it "Untitled" or anything that pops into your head. Then write your byline. Now move on to the dreaded page one. Write FADE IN: (already, your screenplay is in progress). Skip a couple of lines and write anything, *and I do mean anything*, that comes to mind: "Now is the time for all good men . . ." "It's cold out today." "I've got a headache." "I hate doing this exercise." It makes no difference. The only restriction you must accept is that you put this improvised screenplay in standard screenplay form.

As your first step toward becoming a screenwriter, I suggest you buy a few screenplays and study the form. It's simple and quite easy to learn. Screenplays are readily available to anybody, anywhere. (Most large bookstores have published copies of well-known screenplays.) For the purposes of this exercise, the one you choose doesn't matter. However, while you're spending the money, you should pick a screenplay from one of your favorite films for more serious study later. Right now you only need learn the screenplay form.

You don't have to live in an area that has large bookstores. You can write or phone bookstores that specialize in books on films. Two well-known film-specialty bookstores are Samuel French Bookstores, 7623 Sunset Blvd., Hollywood, CA 90046, phone: (213) 876-0570 (they carry many screenplays and can give you their list of what's available) and Larry Edmunds Bookshop, 6644 Hollywood Blvd., Hollywood, CA 90028, phone: (213) 463-3273. Whatever these scripts cost you, they're an inexpensive way to introduce yourself to screenwriting. If you aren't interested enough in the subject to read and study screenplays before you begin to write, you can reasonably assume that you are on the wrong career path. Writing is very hard work and not for the faint of heart or mind.

(*Scenario*, an excellent quarterly magazine, publishes copies of the latest screenplays along with interviews with the authors. Though expensive, *Scenario* will probably prove an excellent investment for you. To subscribe or to order a copy, phone (800) 222-2654.)

Okay, you've bought this book, done some homework, studied a few screenplays, and know screenplay form. (Learning the form will take you less than an hour.)

After you've written your cover sheet, go to the next blank page (page one) and type "1" in the upper right-hand corner of the page. Do not, *do not* be "creative" about where you put your page numbers. They always go in the upper right-hand corner of the page because that is where all professional readers look for them. Page numbers are an instant guide that tells them how many minutes into the movie they are. (The average ratio is about a minute of film per page of script, though this can vary considerably according to the pace of the director and the number of action sequences you've written.)

For this first experimental screenplay, don't spend a lot of time getting the margins or even the spelling perfect; you can do that with your next screenplay. For now, just *make it look like a screenplay*. You are the only one who will ever see it.

Continue to write anything and everything that comes to mind. Put in some character names off the top of your head, and let them say anything, even if all they can talk about is the weather. Just get them talking.

There will be some scenes in which you will want to describe action without dialogue. These scenes have the location and NIGHT or DAY at the top, followed by the letters M.O.S. (This stands for "mit out sound," originally coined by a German cameraman in the very early days of moviemaking.)

Locate your first scene anywhere your imagination takes you: INTERIOR, EXTERIOR, anywhere in the world. Your scenes do not have to be in any preplanned sequence or order. Your spontaneous ideas dictate the next scene and the next. Who knows, a sequence might develop, even a story might develop. If it does, go with it, see where it takes you. Follow it until you decide it doesn't work. When it stops working, abandon it and move on; other ideas, other stories will flash though your mind. Wherever your imagination takes you, follow it, but don't stop writing. Like a jazz musician, you will hit some exciting riffs. No doubt, some interesting characters will come to mind. *Get them down on your pages.* You may very likely want to go back and explore them for another screenplay. That's great. They won't be lost, they're now on the page.

As you write, remember to loosen up, lighten up. This is an exercise. Like stretching before a physical workout, you are stretching your creative muscles. You are warming up to become a screenwriter. All that counts is that you keep writing, putting words on your page, any words, any ideas. You must totally forget any need to succeed, to make this script great, to please anybody, even yourself. The important thing is to keep going. Let your imagination run free; it's exhilarating and liberating. And as Satchel Paige said, "Don't look back, something might be gaining on you."

All art is trial and error—the freedom to work on anything that comes into your head and to turn your imaginings into something you value and want to communicate to others. Improvising is an important aspect of art. Many artists begin to learn their craft by improvising: actors, potters, musicians, dancers, and painters do it.

Once you begin your improvised screenplay and commit yourself to it, ideas will emerge; you can't stop them. Many may be worthless, but some might be wonderful. Forget value judgments, that's not what this is about. Like sewing seeds, you're never certain which ones will bear fruit. But if you don't plant them at all, nothing will grow. Ideas not recorded will vanish. Get them down now—later you will be delighted you have them.

Force yourself into a schedule, just a few hours a day, every day, early in the morning or late at night. Set a goal of five pages a day, seven days a week whenever possible. Once the rhythm of writing becomes a part of your daily life, it will stay with you for a very long time, perhaps for life.

In a matter of weeks you will have your first screenplay; you will see 110 or 120 pages stacked up and, no matter how meaningless it might all be, you will have conquered the greatest fear that writers face—the blank page, especially the blank *first* page. You will come out of this exercise with a real sense of accomplishment, believe me.

Read it over, see if there are any ideas or situations in it that might be worth exploring and developing. Great ideas often come from free association. Make note of these possible nuggets and save them in a file. Then throw the rest of your improvised screenplay into the wastebasket.

You will be surprised by how much you've learned during this exercise. You have learned that you can develop the discipline it takes to be a professional writer—*to do the work, to walk your talk*—and, just as importantly, you have learned how important it may or may not be for you to become a screenwriter.

If you are serious about a screenwriting career, this heavy-duty exercise will produce some surprisingly positive results. There's a very good chance that, while you have been writing gibberish, some workable ideas have taken root in your imagination and on the page. They may grow and lead you to your next screenplay. It happens. One thing is certain: You will never know until you try it.

To be a successful screenwriter you must be driven to be a successful screenwriter. Those who are willing to commit serious time and energy to the work have a chance for success. Others need not apply. You have to keep plugging away, learning by doing: *faking it until you make it.* You must write screenplay after screenplay until you get it right. Most professional writers working today did just that.

And it all begins with letting go of your fear, especially your fear of that intimidating page one. I urge you to put it aside and attack this exercise with a real commitment to your own growth and development. Write your name 100 times, if need be. Write "the little brown fox jumped over the . . ." Just get some words on paper and keep them coming—one word, one sentence at a time. Before you know it, you will have conquered your fear, and putting words on paper will be as natural as breathing. When you fake it till you make it, the fakery slowly disappears and you become the real article—a screenwriter.

Writer's Block

Many successful screenwriters go through painful periods during which, for often inexplicable reasons, they cannot write. Their minds suddenly become empty, their fear of failure suddenly overwhelms them. Alas, this is an all-too-commonplace disease.

Most writers in the throes of writer's block merely wait until it passes. For some it takes months, even years. Like a sailboat becalmed without a breeze, they drift aimlessly, unable to function. Some seek out therapists who specialize in patients with writer's block (in Hollywood and, no doubt, in New York there are licensed therapists, many of them former professional writers themselves, who devote their practices to this frightening writers' malaise). I'm certain that these therapists help many who are caught in the creative doldrums.

If you cannot afford or cannot find a therapist to help you, the best solution is to write your way out of it. Start your recovery with an improvisational screenplay. It might prove to be an important step toward a cure. Simply put your random words in the correct screenplay format, with no expectations, with no fear of failure or judgment. Show it to no one. It is for your eyes only.

The Movie Game

Here's a technique for sharpening your skills as a screenwriting storyteller.

Get together with a few of your fellow aspiring screenwriter friends and improvise a movie. It's surprisingly easy and quite helpful in understanding what goes into writing a film. This is the way I did it in my graduate screenwriting seminars at UCLA:

As the facilitator, I would start The Movie Game by announcing to my student writers, "We're going to create a movie here and now. Everybody is going to contribute as we move along, building our story. The only rule is *you must tell us only what we, the audience, see or hear on the screen; no history, no backstory.*" Then I'd call out, "What's the first scene?"

This always took a bit of prodding because most students are shy about going out on a limb with an idea that could sound crazy. But that's the point: take a chance, get started with any scene that comes into your head. What do we see on the screen at the start of our movie?

The first volunteer finally speaks up: "A large corporate jet is landing at the Mexico City airport. After it pulls to a stop, the doors swing open and a tall, thin, beautiful young woman gets out."

"How old is she?" I ask the student.

"She's twenty-six."

"She's a lawyer," says another student.

"How do we know that?" I ask him.

"She's carrying a large, very heavy legal briefcase."

"Why does that make her a lawyer?" asks another student.

This slows the pace for a moment, so I rush in with my lesson: "As screenwriters we want to hold onto the audience's curiosity as long as possible and we want to guard our surprises, first and foremost. I don't want to know anything about her just yet, except what she looks like. Let's continue. We've got a beautiful woman exiting a corporate jet at the Mexico City airport, carrying a heavy briefcase. That's all we see and that's all we need to know for now. We're naturally curious about her, and so is our audience. What else do we see that helps define her?"

"She's very stylish," says another student, "successful, definitely upscale."

"Let's give her a name," I suggest.

"It's Ashley," says another student. "Ashley Anderson."

"Any objections?" I ask. "Okay, she's Ashley Anderson, let's move on."

"A handsome older guy exits the plane behind her; he's carrying a heavy briefcase, too," says another writer.

"How old is he?" I ask, "and what's our visual impression of him?"

"He's fifty-five, slightly gray, dressed in an English-tailored suit; this guy reeks money, big bucks," says another student. "His name is David Brighton. These two are wheelers and dealers."

"He's her lover," shouts another student.

"No way," responds another, "Ashley is her own woman, she doesn't need to fuck her way to the top."

The Movie Game is underway; everybody is involved in creating our improvised screen story. Writers are leaning forward in their seats trying to figure out the next scene. We are all curious what this story is about and where it's going to lead us. We feel the same way we want the audience to feel: genuinely interested and curious. Several students begin shouting ideas at once.

"Hold on," I tell them, "somebody's going to have to take down the scenes that we all agree we want in our story. I need a volunteer."

One of the writers pulls out a note pad and begins listing our scenes.

What we're doing here is building what I call a "rising action" story, a causes-and-effects drama. Each scene is an event that leads us to the next scene or event. We have a storyline going for us or, as I prefer to call it, an *"action line."* Action is the key word for all drama (our word "drama" derives from the Greek "drâma" meaning "to do, to take action").

"Okay," I tell them, "we've got an interesting opening, an arrival, but we need more, and soon. Where's the conflict in this story? Where's the dramatic tension coming from? What's going to be *the problem*? You can't begin to build dramatic tension too soon. Let's hook our audience."

Another student jumps in, "There's a young Mexican guy in a limo waiting at the bottom of the jet stairs, and he's on a cellular phone telling somebody, 'They're here, I'll bring them right away.' He's low-key but we see sinister ideas on his face. On the seat, tucked just under his thigh, we can see the barrel of a gun, an Uzi. They enter the car without seeing the gun; it's well hidden."

"In the backseat of the limo as they drive into Mexico City, Ashley and David are making brief comments on the strategy they plan to use to make the financial deal they're negotiating with the Mexican government," another student suggests. "This is a very big deal. Now we learn she's a lawyer specializing in international banking. Very few comments—we keep the dialogue lean and mean."

This gets a laugh from the group because that is what I tell my students their dialogue should be, unless there is a Paddy Chayefsky or a Rod Serling among them.

"What kind of relationship are we seeing between these two people?" I ask. I want to keep pushing the story along, keep everybody involved, focused, and in the process.

"Strictly business," says a student, "but he'd like to get in her pants."

"Is she interested? You can't write a scene unless you know the attitude of all the characters in it. Does she want to have sex with him?" I ask.

"Definitely not," says another student, "this woman knows how to use her sexuality when she wants to, but she doesn't let it get in the way of her work. She's in control."

"What's the limo driver up to?" I ask them.

"He's a young guy, good looking, high cheek bones, Mexican-Indian. He's got another agenda, but we don't know what his deal is."

"Okay, we've got a story started that we can work with: good characters, an early start of dramatic tension, and a strong situation. What's next?" I ask.

"'Driver, take us to the presidential palace, please,' David tells the driver."

"The driver turns toward them as he drives, 'Be careful, my friends,' he says in perfect English, 'you may be making a deal with the devil.'"

"'The president of Mexico is a devil?' David replies," says another student.

"'Yes,' the driver says, 'There will be a revolution soon.'"

Now everybody is into it, we are all caught up in our own movie, and it's fair to say that all of us want to know what's going to happen next. As in all stories, curiosity is the writer's best weapon. (During the development of your *story,* you, the screenwriter, want to know what's going to happen next. That's the fuel that keeps you going.)

Our game is not only afoot, it is moving forward with its own momentum. The screenwriters are beginning to build their own story, arguing over scenes, getting excited as this story seems to un-fold, almost magically, by itself. I intervene only when somebody interjects background information. I insist that we only create scenes that the audience will see on the screen. What our audience doesn't know is our greatest weapon—we must hold onto this curiosity as long as possible and try to keep building on it.

When we all know we've got something we want to work on, I remind everyone, "This is a group effort. Whatever we finally come up with belongs to all of you to use as you see fit. I'm the facilitator—my job is to keep you on track, not to write your story for you."

I prod my writers on for as long as their story can hold their interest; sometimes we give up after the first ten or fifteen scenes, sometimes we go on to as many as thirty or forty. Length is not important. The importance of The Movie Game is the lessons the writers learn as we create a movie story and solve the same kinds of problems we, as writers, all face when we're trying to create a story for ourselves.

The feedback I've gotten on The Movie Game, from Copenhagen to Honolulu to Melbourne, has consistently been enthusiastic and positive; writers feel they learn both the pitfalls of creating stories and the elements needed to make a story work.

You don't have to be a UCLA graduate student, or even be in a classroom, to practice, develop, and hone your skills as film storytellers. Any small group of writers can get together and work on their storytelling skills, and on their own stories, while playing The Movie Game. You should have somebody who will act as a facilitator—an outside observer, a referee to keep it moving and to keep it from going astray. A word of warning: If you've seen the story before or if the scenes are familiar, reject them. Insist that the writers come up with a fresh approach. No matter how old the idea may be, you've got to make it new.

• • • • •

I once tried The Movie Game with a class of twenty students and quickly realized it wasn't feasible. With too many people throwing out ideas simultaneously, it quickly became unmanageable. Experience has taught me that five or six writers is the ideal number.

I suggest you organize your own small writers' group of a half-dozen or less who will meet weekly, playing The Movie Game, developing stories for the screen. You will be surprised how quickly you will sharpen your skill at telling film stories.

And just as importantly, you will quickly realize how much help you can be to one another. Screenwriters helping fellow screenwriters is the best way there is to learn screenwriting. Which is, of course, why the first rule I gave myself when I reorganized the UCLA screenwriting program was that I would only hire working screenwriters as teachers. It is my absolute conviction that screenwriters are best qualified to teach screenwriters, as musicians are best qualified to teach musicians. Would Julliard hire a non-playing musician to teach clarinet? In my opinion, the UCLA screenwriting program is the Julliard of screenwriting schools.

A surprising result of The Movie Game was that, in one instance, some years back, three of my students took the story we were creating in our seminar and, with the permission of the rest of the class, continued to work on it during the summer after they graduated. They changed it, revised it considerably, until it bore little relationship to the initial improvised story, which was the seed from which they finally completed a screenplay. Then they went out and got their own financing, shot their film in Mexico, and began their careers, two as screenwriters, one as a producer. They are still close friends and two of them still collaborate.

The Movie Game has been an enthusiastic success in every screenwriting seminar I've ever taught. It primes the creative pump, it help writers get over the fear of the dreaded blank page. If you're stuck on which story idea to go with, form a small group of fellow writers and play The Movie Game. Chances are that your ability to tell a movie story will grow considerably. Whenever you are stuck on a story, never hesitate to seek help from fellow writers. Nothing is better for you than batting ideas around with your peers, writers who've shared your frustrations and fears. We are all in this endeavor together and nobody ever told us it was going to be easy.

How To Get There From Here

Everybody, without exception, has creativity in one area or another, to one degree or another. We are all born with this gift. The goal for aspiring screenwriters and all other artists is to find and develop that creativity.

Creativity is spontaneity. It's the freedom to explore any idea that your mind can conceive without restrictions. Anybody who gives you rules or advice before you create will restrict the flow of your creativity as a clamp would restrict the flow of your blood. Rules are the enemy of creativity and will shut it down faster than a speeding bullet.

When asked how he went about writing, William Faulkner is said to have responded, "I see these characters running down the road and I follow them with pencil or pen." Nobody told Mr. Faulkner that you really can't do it like that, you first have to learn structure. Yet he managed to win the Nobel Prize for Literature by going his own way, following his instincts as a storyteller.

Dr. Annette Covatta, in her excellent seminar on Releasing Your Creative Energies, points out that creativity arises out of chaos. She also suggests that the key aspects of creativity are (1) challenging assumptions, (2) seeing in a new way, (3) making connections, and (4) taking risks.

One of the good doctor's recommendations is to use music to awaken and free your creativity. She uses Smetana's *The Moldau* as an example of creatively inspirational music. I know of professional writers who keep music playing as they write. They prefer music that does not distract, that serves as a comforting backdrop to support and encourage the free flow of ideas. I suggest that "classical" music playing at an unobtrusive level is very good to help you let your creativity flow freely. On the other hand, some writers use loud rock music to put them in the mood. To each his own.

Music not only has the power to bring out your creativity, it also keeps you company during difficult and lonely hours. There will be times when you will want to simply drift with it, letting yourself go, which is a very good idea. In spite of your drifting, ideas for your work will continue to flow.

History tells us that several famous writers used hallucinogens to free their creativity. I personally don't recommend getting stoned out of your head in order to write, not on moral grounds but on my belief that an altered state of mind alters your judgment of what is good and what is gibberish. I've known writers who've used the method with success and others who have produced nothing worthwhile while under the influence. I believe the latter is the most likely result, and I urge you to keep your wits about you while you work.

Everybody has their own method to evoke the Muse. You've got a Muse; use whatever it takes to help guide your words—whatever works for you. The tool you choose is unimportant. Taking the risk and doing it is what counts.

Your business as a writer is not to illustrate virtue but to show how a fellow may move toward it or away from it.
—Robert Penn Warren, from *Paris Review, 1957*

. . . [the writer] must teach himself that the basest of all things is to be afraid and, teaching himself that, forget it forever, leaving no room in his workshop for anything but the old verities and truths of the heart, the universal truths lacking which any story is ephemeral and doomed—love and horror and pity and pride and compassion and sacrifice.
—William Faulkner, Nobel Prize Speech

The whole duty of a writer is to satisfy himself, and the true writer plays to an audience of one.
—E.B. White

Sometimes A Really Great Notion

An Interview with

Callie Khouri

"Resistance to your work is an obstacle, but it isn't an obstacle that can't be overcome. Tenacity is probably one of the most important characteristics that you can have. You have to have the same tenacity toward your work as you expect other people to have toward it. You may have to write and rewrite a scene fifteen times before it's really good. And you may have to write fifteen scripts before somebody likes one. If you want to be a screenwriter, that's what you've got to do."

—Callie Khouri

Callie Khouri is one of the outstanding screenwriters of her generation. With her very first screenplay, she exploded on both the Hollywood and the international film scene. *Thelma and Louise* was more than a breakthrough movie: it was a powerful, dynamic, feminist statement that won the hearts of critics and audiences (both male and female) alike. She dramatized her theme of women seeking freedom from their difficult life situations with such skill, suspense, humor, and command of her medium that only the most die-hard anti-feminist could object to it. She created two characters who were fascinating, yet ordinary and identifiable. You could not help but cheer them on.

The Motion Picture Academy of Arts and Sciences awarded Callie Khouri an Oscar for Best Original Screenplay, and the Writers Guild of America also presented her with their Best Original Screenplay award. And many more awards and honors followed.

Callie Khouri's second original story and screenplay, *Something to Talk About*, was produced in 1995.

This remarkable screenwriter is batting 1.000. Two screenplays written, two sold; the first a classic and the second all class. But Ms. Khouri is not a writer to rest on her laurels. She turned her considerably energy and talents to "gender politics," serving on the board of the California Abortion and Reproductive Rights Action League. (She frequently speaks on reproductive rights.) In 1991 she received a Feminist of the Year Award from the Feminist Majority Foundation, and in 1992 she was the recipient of the Second Annual Los Angeles Women Making

History Award and the New York Women in Communications Matrix Award. Small wonder there was a five-year gap between her debut film, *Thelma and Louise*, and *Something to Talk About*.

Our conversation was laced with laughter and good humor. Callie Khouri is a most delightful woman to talk to, managing to be both serious and funny at the same time, just like Thelma and Louise. She is not only a writer to talk about, she is also a writer to listen to.

FROUG: I rented *Thelma and Louise* this weekend and I was astonished by how current it is. It's ageless. Do you think anything has changed much, vis-à-vis the societal position of women, during the five years since you wrote *Thelma and Louise*?

KHOURI: I don't know. I've come to expect only baby steps, and those are so hard to judge. I guess we've come some way—there was a flap that didn't go away over Bob Packwood remaining in the Senate. But, you know, Clarence Thomas is sitting on the Supreme Court. And O.J. Simpson walks free. There is some indication that things have not really taken a quantum leap forward. But, I like to remain optimistic. I think that, this year, we saw a lot more women get movies made.

FROUG: That's good news. Has there been any advancement in the employment of women as screenwriters?

KHOURI: I hope so. But it's harder on women writers. I don't think it's gonna help anybody if they have a lackluster performance at the box office. For some reason, you can have a lackluster box

"For some reason, you can have a lackluster box office for a Sylvester Stallone movie, or a Baldwin brothers movie, and that doesn't seem to indicate any kind of trend. But if a woman's movie fails, then that's a blanket audience rejection of the whole genre, in the studio's mind."

office for a Sylvester Stallone movie, or a Baldwin brothers movie, and that doesn't seem to indicate any kind of trend. But if a woman's movie fails, then that's a blanket audience rejection of the whole genre, in the studio's mind.

FROUG: The problem has always been that the studios are desperately searching for the sure-fire formula for success. If anything goes awry, they say, "Let's stay away from that, that formula didn't work."

KHOURI: It is like an alchemical equation, and you really can't say why one may succeed and one may fail. I've seen plenty of movies that I thought were terrible do incredible business. Obviously, the ones that are not action-oriented are not going to have the foreign audience. Action-oriented movies can flop here and still manage to drum up big business overseas.

FROUG: Were you surprised by the reaction *Thelma and Louise* got?

KHOURI: I was just thrilled by the positive reaction and stunned by the negative reaction because I did not for a moment see the movie as male bashing.

FROUG: Neither did I.

KHOURI: What is interesting or enlightening about it is that when you show men as secondary characters, a certain fragment of the male population has a very difficult time with that concept. I've had a lot of guys come up to me and say, "I wanted to know more about Darryl, Thelma's husband."

FROUG: The movie wasn't about him.

KHOURI: I know—there are trillions of movies already out there about that guy. But if you have problems with the way certain men in the movie have been represented, read the script and see the way the characters were portrayed there. You'll notice a big difference between the performances and what I had in mind.

FROUG: For example?

KHOURI: A choice was made by the director, and by the actors, that portrayed the men in a way that even I felt was extreme. The director was really going straight for comedy with the truck driver and with the character of Darryl, whom I always thought of as comic but not cartoonish.

FROUG: I had forgotten how much humor there is in *Thelma and Louise*.

KHOURI: I can't imagine writing a movie that doesn't have at least a few good laughs in it. You know, at least a smile. I insist on being entertained when I go to a movie theater.

FROUG: I think that is a very special talent. Not many writers are able to suddenly cross over from dramatic intensity to comedy.

KHOURI: It seems that life is so much like that.

FROUG: What did you do during the five years between writing *Thelma and Louise* and *Something to Talk About*?

KHOURI: I was actually writing that second script the whole time. I had a very difficult time after *Thelma and Louise* came out. When I started writing my next script, I wasn't sure exactly what I wanted to say. I kind of got off on the wrong direction with the character of Grace. And there was a presidential election during that period, so I took a lot of time out to campaign. I also got married and bought a house the week the film started shooting. I was going through a major life change. And it took a few years to get things settled down. I finished

"I can't imagine writing a movie that doesn't have at least a few good laughs in it."

the screenplay of *Something to Talk About* in January of '94, and we started shooting it in November of the same year.

I think *Something to Talk About* was a good second film for me in terms of trying to do something more challenging with structure. My screenplay is all character-driven. You can't really write scenes ahead, because you have to know the exact emotional state the characters are going to be in when they get there. The events that precede a scene have to get them to a certain place. So even though I knew things that I wanted to have happen ahead of time—like I wanted Grace to stand up at the woman's meeting and say, "Who else here has fucked my husband?"—I had to wait until I got there to actually write those scenes.

FROUG: Do you outline before you start to write?

KHOURI: I did on *Something to Talk About*. I did not on *Thelma and Louise*.

FROUG: How detailed are your outlines?

KHOURI: I do cards for every scene.

FROUG: You use scene-card technique?

KHOURI: I did on *Something to Talk About*. Actually, it didn't start out that way, but once I got into it, I had to do something because it was too confusing—I couldn't keep track. The scene cards allowed me to see whether the problems were with the order of the scenes or with the characters. Scene cards illuminated a lot of things. When I wrote *Thelma and Louise*, I just started and wrote toward the end.

FROUG: Well, you had an action-driven movie.

KHOURI: Right. It was a very straight-line structure, and *Something to Talk About* was a more circular structure.

FROUG: To me, *Something to Talk About* shows a more mature writer at work.

KHOURI: I truly hope so. I'm always thinking, oh my God, who am I trying to kid?

FROUG: I read reviews of *Something to Talk About* that shocked me. Some reviewers must have gone to a different movie than the one I saw.

KHOURI: Well, I think some people walk into a movie theater with chips on their shoulders. I don't know. I think that a critic's job is that of a eunuch at an orgy. I read a few bad reviews, which I kind of ignored to tell you the truth. I don't care about pleasing everybody. There's a certain group of people that I hope will tell their friends about the film. I went to see the movie in the theater one night, and there was a guy in front of me who I thought was going to have to be carried out on a stretcher.

FROUG: Laughing so hard?

KHOURI: Laughing so hard. And, you know, if you had looked at him, you would have thought that there's nothing in this movie for this kind of guy. And next to me was a woman who I thought was going to love the movie, and she didn't crack a smile one single time.

FROUG: The audience remains unpredictable. I think that's to our benefit.

KHOURI: Yeah.

FROUG: A lot of team writing is going on nowadays. Have you joined the rewrite industry?

"I think that a critic's job is that of a eunuch at an orgy."

"I think a lot of the movies we are seeing now are Frankenstein monsters— they've had parts donated from all over the place, they don't really add up to a whole thing."

KHOURI: No, I haven't. I don't know that I have much of a facility for that, and I certainly don't have a tremendous amount of interest in it. I guess that if I really needed the money, I would do it. And I could probably be somewhat helpful, but I'm always so shocked that anybody could have an idea at all to begin with that I'm pretty much awe-struck if it's a *good* idea. If it's a bad idea, it makes me mad that somebody wants to make the movie in spite of it—that they think you can take a bad idea and make it good. I use the analogy that a story is a whole thing, like a human being is a whole person. You can't just make a person by taking an arm here and a leg there and a torso here, put them all together, and expect to have a human being. Yet that methodology is applied to screenplays.

I think a lot of the movies we are seeing now are Frankenstein monsters—they've had parts donated from all over the place, they don't really add up to a whole thing.

FROUG: That may be because of the proliferating business of hiring rewriter after rewriter after rewriter. There is a story in this book that was told to me by my former student Laurence Dworet, who sold a screenplay for a picture called *Outbreak*. Another former UCLA screenwriting student did nineteen weeks of rewriting on it for $60,000 a week, and they didn't use a line of what that rewriter wrote.

KHOURI: I've heard stories that would curl your hair. Stories of writers who are paid $300,000 to do a rewrite and end up with one line in the movie. I say, hey, give me that money, let it sustain me for a period of years, and I'll turn out one script every four years. And, by God, I promise you it will be good.

FROUG: It must be the panic over the current huge budgets. The studios must be desperately trying to make certain that each movie is going to be a hit.

KHOURI: A hundred thousand dollars a week for rewriters, when you're paying an actor twenty million dollars, doesn't really seem like very much. Actors are getting deals for twenty million dollars now, *plus* a percentage of the gross. Star salaries have become absurd. A hundred thousand dollars a week for a rewriter becomes chump change by comparison.

FROUG: Do you think that pay television and cable are going to offer an alternative market that will provide work for more writers?

KHOURI: I think it's happening already. You know, HBO and Showtime are doing original movies, and the networks have to become more competitive.

FROUG: Do you think that will also be a boon for women writers?

KHOURI: I hope so. I'm endlessly optimistic. But as long as violence and sex are the hottest-selling ticket, I doubt that women are gonna be making great strides, because we're not schooled in violence in the same way men are.

FROUG: Let's hope you never get schooled.

KHOURI: Yeah. There's a lot of violence specifically directed to a male audience, things that have a certain amount of appeal to their base instincts. But it's not there for women. There's not violence that's specifically directed to a female audience. I think that *Thelma and Louise* had a kind of violence, even though I don't think of it as violence. Even blowing up the truck wasn't

"Star salaries have become absurd. A hundred thousand dollars a week for a rewriter becomes chump change by comparison."

really violent. The way they took the driver out of the truck—they didn't kill him, they didn't shoot him in the knee. You see those kinds of things in other movies all the time. I was shocked to hear *Thelma and Louise* referred to as violent.

FROUG: You didn't need to resort to violence because you had two characters running for their lives. That's a very strong line of action.

KHOURI: The script was fully written before anybody saw it, and it only changed minutely by the time it got to the screen.

FROUG: How many years did it take you to sell it?

KHOURI: It didn't take a year. I finished it in August and by January we were going to do it.

FROUG: How long had you worked on it?

KHOURI: Six months.

FROUG: What was the seed of that movie? Where did it spring from?

KHOURI: I had been doing a lot of work in music videos. I don't think that there is a lower life form on the film chain. Even though there are plenty of women working in production, the way women are represented in music videos is the absolute bottom. After several years, I found that completely depressing. I had to get myself right with the universe again. My gender politics. So when I decided I was gonna start writing, I had to pick something to balance all the years I had spent working in that machine. I wanted it to be a movie about women who felt a certain way. The feeling of becoming, just busting out free into the world. I was driving home one night from a shoot and I pulled up in front of my house and I had a thought: What would it be like if two women went out on a crime spree? I knew that that was it, and the whole thing kind of flashed before my eyes.

FROUG: Amazing. Did you know who the women were?

KHOURI: No, I didn't. I just had a lot of questions after that, but I saw this kind of incredible transformation of two women. Then I started asking: Why would they go on a crime spree? What would that be like? What two women would go on a crime spree? What would drive them to go on? And I wanted positive women—women who had problems and weren't perfect, but weren't evil and manipulative and psychotic. So, basically, two average women end up on a crime spree. Obviously, the possibilities are endless. It was something that I couldn't distinctly remember ever having seen before. And it wasn't overly sexualized. I thought, they're not going to be prostitutes. If you would go to any number of male studio executives, they'd say, "Let's do a movie about women criminals," and they would start with prostitution. I wanted to do something that was completely different from that.

FROUG: So you came up with something totally original.

KHOURI: I tried.

FROUG: You must have succeeded because it was an enormous success, wasn't it?

KHOURI: It was. It went really well.

FROUG: Did you like the casting?

KHOURI: I loved it.

FROUG: Did you have any idea that Brad Pitt was going to become a superstar one day?

KHOURI: Well, I don't know if we knew that, but everybody was extremely, extremely enthusiastic about Brad Pitt, and we really did look long and hard. In fact, they came extremely close to casting Billy Baldwin in it, but he backed out.

FROUG: Just a case of luck, I guess.

KHOURI: Yeah. It was really a fortunate thing all the way around.

FROUG: When you're writing, when you're really cooking, how many pages a day do you hope to get?

KHOURI: It depends. On a good day, it's six pages. Some days, it's one page. But if it's a good page, that's okay. I try not to put any unobtainable goals in front of myself. I never think I'm gonna write eight pages a day. If I can get between three and five pages, I'm happy. Basically, I want to come out of the day with a scene.

FROUG: About how many hours a day do you try to average?

KHOURI: Well, I'm one of those who, if it's there, can sit and write all day. If not, I can script fifteen minutes and know I gotta go.

FROUG: Are you a morning person or a night person?

KHOURI: Both. It depends on what scene I'm writing. Sometimes I feel like there are certain scenes that I have to write in the middle of the night. And sometimes, I get up at five o'clock in the morning and want to write. Sometimes I wake up in the middle of the night and write something down that I don't work on until four o'clock the next afternoon. If I know I've got it, then I don't worry about it.

FROUG: Do you toss around sometimes with scenes spinning in your head when you're trying to sleep?

KHOURI: Yes, I've had certain times when I think, okay, I cannot let this pass, I've got to write it down, I'm not gonna remember it. I always make sure that I don't make the mistake of thinking it will be there in the morning. I get up and write it. Even if it's dumb or awful or bad, I get it down on paper.

FROUG: Do you use a computer?

KHOURI: I use Movie Master.

FROUG: That's a program that automatically puts your work in screenplay form?

KHOURI: Right.

FROUG: Do you generally try for a three-act structure? Do you pay any attention to that?

KHOURI: Well, I don't really pay any attention to it. I had a wonderful guy, Jim Rogers, who helped me on this last movie. A writer friend of mine told me about him. When my friend got really hung up, he had Jim come talk to him and help him. One of the things that Jim did for me was tell me that I had a five-act structure, and that's why I was getting confused about the three acts. He told me to forget about it. And so I did. It's really helpful not to have to think like that about a movie. I try to make sure that I know the pace that I want the movie to have, and know the feeling that I want the movie to have. I try not to weigh myself down with any rules.

FROUG: Have you gone to any of those weekend guru sessions?

KHOURI: No, I haven't. I've looked at some of the books and I think that some of them are probably incredibly helpful. At the same time, I see scripts where I can tell that somebody had read this book or that book. And, on page twenty-three, sure enough . . .

"I try not to weigh myself down with any rules."

FROUG: There's the phrase "turning point," right?

KHOURI: Right. You need an organic feeling to the script, whether it's the most surreal thing in the world or the most realistic thing in the world. It has to have its own life, and I don't think you can impose that on it with outside formulas.

FROUG: Some of these self-styled story-structure gurus seem to be saying that that's what you should do. Of course, few if any of them are screenwriters.

KHOURI: The thing that's interesting to me about this, Bill, is that screenwriting seems to be the only form of writing where the general perception is that anybody can do it. I don't think that anybody can write a short story or that anybody can write a novel. But the idea that any clown can pick up one of these books and then go out and write a screenplay that's gonna get sold is incredible. The unfortunate thing is that a lot of clowns do write screenplays that get sold. And a lot of crummy movies get made on top of it. I'm sure that a lot of crummy short stories and a lot of crummy novels get written, too, but I haven't come across thousands of books about how anybody can become a novelist or a great short-story writer in five easy steps.

There are rules for any kind of writing, but they're just conventional wisdom. Just because somebody has seen movies, they say, I can do that. I don't know why they don't have the same feelings about other kinds of writing. I think it's very, very confusing to the people who are following all these screenwriting steps. How come their scripts aren't any good? Well, maybe they just can't write. Do they ever think of that? They don't think of that. I read scripts with dialogue that is so bad and action that is so boring and plots that are nonexistent. Well, nobody ever remembers the plot anyway. We remember the characters, and that's what you have to have happen.

I was just at this screenwriters' conference in Austin, Texas. It was really great. I did a panel with Scott Frank, Frank Pierson, Ed Solomon, and Shane Black. We were having a big old time and somebody commented, "It's not rocket science." And I said, "It is rocket science. It's exactly like rocket science— all this work that has to go into it, all these little problems that have to be worked out. Sometimes there's one problem that can hang you up for years. You may have to expend all your energy working out one little thing. Until that's solved, the whole thing won't fly." The idea that it's something simple that a moron can do is just wrong. I'm sure some self-deprecating writers will say that it's not that hard, but I have to disagree. Good writing is difficult for even the best writers.

FROUG: Some of the best writers struggle for years to get one good script out, as you did with *Something to Talk About*. By the way, where did you get that title?

KHOURI: It was called that by the marketing people at Warner Bros. My original title was *Grace Under Pressure*. But they wouldn't use it, so I said what about *Saving Grace*? But they wouldn't do that either. They came up with *Something to Talk About* because it was a Bonnie Raitt song. The song didn't really have anything to do with the movie. The song is about an office romance, an illicit affair.

FROUG: Did *Something to Talk About* do well?

KHOURI: Yeah, it did.

FROUG: Do you know what it cost to make?

KHOURI: Forty million. So far it's grossed over fifty million.

FROUG: So it'll wind up in profit?

KHOURI: Yes, it will.

FROUG: But you'll never see a penny of your percentage points, I assume.

KHOURI: Oh, no, no, no. It works like this: The studio says, "We'll take thirty percent of the profit right off the top, and then every expense we'll charge against your share of the profit." I think that this would be unheard of in any other kind of business. We should change that.

FROUG: Didn't Warren Beatty sue Disney on that issue? I read that Jim Garner sued Universal on their definition of distribution costs on *Rockford Files*.

KHOURI: But those are individuals suing a company. If I were going to do it, I would try to get a bunch of other people to do it with me, because a studio has a legal team in place. They can spend years and years and years on it. An individual can't spend years and years and years on it unless they're already extremely rich, at which point they'd have to ask themselves whether it's worth it. Am I going to spend more than I would make? It's completely mind-boggling.

FROUG: People who never see a dime of their "points," as the industry calls the pieces of profit, even when their movie does blockbuster business, are driven crazy by it. But I don't think many people have ever beaten the system.

KHOURI: I've also seen a terrible salary turn. I simply would never want to make a movie with somebody who gets five million dollars. I just don't think it's worth it.

FROUG: It's ridiculous. Sylvester Stallone's latest movie, for which he was reportedly paid twenty million dollars, went right down the toilet.

KHOURI: It's the worst thing that could happen in moviemaking. You have absolutely no leeway. But those kinds of movies are not really what I'm interested in anyway. Those are products, and I'm not really that excited about producing products. I want to make somebody a really nice dinner, I don't want to go down to McDonald's. When business people start getting really involved in the creative questions, I always ask if they are going to let writers run the studio for a couple of weeks. They're not, are they? Because I don't have any experience or knowledge or expertise in their area.

FROUG: But they know how to write a screenplay better than you do. That they'll tell you.

KHOURI: Oh, yes.

FROUG: Do you have some suggestions for the young people who will read this book on how to go about becoming a screen-writer?

KHOURI: I watched every movie I could watch until I found a profound appreciation of just what it was that the screenwriter did.

FROUG: I highly recommend the same. Study as many movies as you possibly can.

KHOURI: I had also studied acting. I was a drama major in college.

FROUG: Where did you go to college?

KHOURI: I went to Purdue. Then I studied acting out here at the Strasberg Institute. And then I worked in production for a number of years. By the time I sat down to write, I was intimately familiar with how an image has gotten to the screen and what the process is for the actor who's going to play it. It's not just about writing and watching movies, it's about making yourself aware of every aspect of what it's gonna take to turn it into an actual movie. It's one thing to sit in a room alone and write a book, because that's where a book is going to be read. It's not going to be read in an auditorium full of people except on a few rare occasions. But a movie is meant to be seen in a group setting, and it's made by large groups of people. It's a very public process. And I think becoming intimately familiar with this process is really, really helpful.

FROUG: How long did it take you to get an agent?

KHOURI: I got an agent almost right away, which was great.

FROUG: With your screenplay *Thelma and Louise*?

KHOURI: Yes.

FROUG: Would you suggest the usual procedure for beginners—writing show scripts?

KHOURI: Yes. I don't think that there's any reason for an agent to take on a client who's never written anything.

FROUG: Do you think that there are openings now for young screenwriters?

KHOURI: Absolutely. If you're driven to do it, you can't take no for an answer. You just have to keep plugging away, regardless of the difficulties you'll face.

FROUG: You are talking about overcoming obstacles.

KHOURI: Right. Resistance to your work is an obstacle, but it isn't an obstacle that can't be overcome. Tenacity is probably one of the most important characteristics that you can have. You have to have the same tenacity toward your work as you expect other people to have toward it. You may have to write and rewrite a scene fifteen times before it's really good. And you may have to write fifteen scripts before somebody likes one. If you want to be a screenwriter that's what you've got to do. I was fortunate because my first script was recognized in the way that it was. Many years of preparation, many years of experience went into that work. But it was something that I had always wanted to do. I had always hoped that I could be a writer.

FROUG: How young were you when you started writing?

KHOURI: I didn't start writing until I was in my late twenties. And I wasn't sure that I could write at all. I was really afraid. But, because of my years of studying acting, I came to realize that there are not many good scripts out there. A lot of people get into acting because they feel very passionately about wanting to do and say something important. They want to cause people to feel. They want to really give something to an audience. If they don't have the words to say, what are they gonna do? I became rather disappointed. During all those years, I wasn't reading a lot of things that I had a burning desire to give to an audience.

FROUG: Well, you had the most extraordinary start imaginable.

KHOURI: I did. I always say, "Don't go by me; it's really hard."

FROUG: Don't kid me, Callie Khouri. You just sit down, write your first script, you sell it, and it becomes a classic. It's that easy.

KHOURI: Yeah. Anybody can do it.

FROUG: [Laughter] Anybody can do it.

CREDITS

Thelma and Louise, 1990 (original story and screenplay)
Also co-producer. Academy Award, WGA Award
"Best Original Screenplay," Golden Globe Award,
PEN Literary Award, London Film Critics Circle
Award for "Film Of The Year."

Something to Talk About, 1995 (original story and screenplay)
Also co-producer.

A World-Class Thoroughbred, a Sure Winner

An Interview with

Eric Roth

"The greatest thing about writing is that you get to enter a whole world where you've never been before."
—Eric Roth

Eric Roth was born with a silver screenplay in his mouth, or then again, several that were pure gold. He is the son of Leon Roth, a former producer (*The Luck of Ginger Coffey*, etc.), Vice President of the Mirisch Company (the most successful independent motion-picture company of the '50s: *Some Like It Hot*, *The Apartment*, *The Great Escape*, *In the Heat of the Night*, *West Side Story*, etc.), and presently a professor at USC's School of Film and Television. Eric's mother is Mimi Roth, writer and former Executive Story Editor at United Artists, a screenwriting teacher at the American Film Institute, a screenwriter's agent, and presently a teacher with UCLA's screenwriting extension program. His parents are among the most informed, intelligent, knowledgeable, and sophisticated people in the Hollywood motion-picture community. Mimi and Leon have been my close friends for well over forty years. It's a friendship I cherish as dearly as any I struck up during my forty years as a writer-producer-teacher in that bizarre, arcane, insane, frustrating, and occasionally satisfying world of Hollywood.

Yet when a tall, good-looking young man in his twenties ambled into my UCLA office one day in 1971, I did not connect him to Mimi and Leon. He was just another student applying to work with me. He handed me a screenplay as his ticket for admission, and we chatted briefly. That evening, I read *Fifty/Fifty* by Eric Roth. It was far and away the best student screenplay I'd ever encountered. It was brilliant. I knew at once that I had nothing to teach Eric, that my job would be simply to get out of his way and watch him rocket to fame and fortune.

His *Fifty/Fifty* screenplay was bought by 20th Century-Fox for director Robert Mulligan. For reasons only they can comprehend, they took the story of a numbers runner in Brooklyn who, facing his fiftieth birthday, was haunted by the disturbing awareness that death would come on the other side of that birthday. He imagined he was being followed by a black-robed man wearing a Puritan hat. (Was the mob out to get him or was he imagining it?) It was a remarkably mature piece of writing. Eric and I discussed Robert Mitchum, who would have been perfect casting at the time. For reasons that defy all understanding, Fox and Mulligan cast a handsome young actor in the leading role, threw out the theme, the concept, and all the story's meaning. They changed the title to *Nickel Ride,* which, as it turned out, was as meaningless as what remained of the gutted screenplay. The picture went "from the projection booth into the toilet," as they say in Hollywood.

Mimi, Leon, Eric, and I went together to the preview screening at Fox. I was dumbstruck and outraged by what they had done to *my* student's work. How dare they! Mimi, Leon, and Eric were remarkably sanguine about the savaging of Eric's first produced screenplay. They were far more Hollywood savvy than I was.

Soon thereafter, Eric moved his young family to Del Mar, California, where the Del Mar race track is located. Though he became an almost daily visitor to the track and trained himself to become a successful handicapper of thoroughbreds ("He got it from both his father and his grandfather," Mimi recently told me), he remained devoted to his screenwriting. He accepted a contract at Universal Studios, where he made a good, if not spectacular, income turning out routine melodramas, and continued to write his own screenplays on the side.

The word got around that Eric Roth was a young screenwriter worth keeping an eye on. He proved that the best revenge is being too talented to be denied. A few more of his screenplays were savaged by lesser talents (*Mr. Jones,* for example), but he was undeterred. As the history of Hollywood proves again and again, nothing and nobody can stop a truly gifted artist determined to follow his or her own vision.

Eric Roth's Oscar for his *Forrest Gump* screenplay came as no surprise. It was long overdue and it will likely be the first of several more.

I was delighted when Eric phoned me the day he received my letter requesting an interview and we immediately and comfortably launched into our taped conversation—two old friends talking about a subject of mutual lifelong interest: screenwriting.

FROUG: Did you expect *Forrest Gump* to be the big hit it turned out to be?

ROTH: No, obviously not. Though I'll tell you quite immodestly, I thought the screenplay was terrific, Tom Hanks thought it was terrific, and Bob Zemeckis thought it was terrific. While we were making the movie, we all felt we had something pretty unique, but we didn't know if we were just drunk and nobody else was.

FROUG: There's a story about Abe Burrows: after the dress rehearsal of the first Broadway production of *Guys and Dolls*, for which he wrote the book, he said to the producer, director, et al., "Who's gonna pay to see this shit?"

ROTH: Interestingly, the very first scene of *Gump* that Bob shot was horrible—the scene was badly written, the performances were bad, I'm not even sure it was very well shot or directed. We looked at the dailies and said, "If this is how the movie is going to be, we're in deep trouble." It was, I think, the only bad scene.

I had some others that could have gone different ways, but that was the only scene that I think was bad, and he threw it out.

FROUG: Was Hanks into that character immediately?

ROTH: No, he wasn't. But Bob Zemeckis was right on—he had an idea of how he even wanted the narration to work and he really studied narration techniques in movies: *Amadeus*, *JFK*, a bunch of movies where it worked successfully. And he decided early on that he was going to tape the narration before we started shooting, use it as bridges while they were filming, then redo the narration after the film was shot as if he was doing one whole scene sitting on the bus bench. So he shot it all. And then he shot the whole narration sitting on the bench after the movie was completed, even though eighty percent was only voice-over.

FROUG: So he could cut in and out when he needed to?

ROTH: The point is that Tom, the first time we went in to do this narration, was just playing around with a southern accent. He sounded like Tom Hanks with a southern accent, he had no real idea who the character was at that point. There was a little boy who was cast as him when he was a little boy who had this strange accent, this little holler Mississippi accent, and Tom kind of duplicated how he sounded. The kid was kind of goofy; I'm not sure whether he had a missing link there somehow.

FROUG: The kid may have been a young Gump.

ROTH: He was a real young Gump. It was a little bit brave on Bob's part because the kid had never acted before. But Tom spent a few days with this boy, and this was the personality he took on.

FROUG: You were what, the third or fourth writer on this attempt to make a movie out of the book?

ROTH: I guess I was the fourth. I have to be honest, I never read any of the previous scripts. I came on probably seven years after the last script was written.

FROUG: The producer was just not able to get something she liked?

ROTH: Wendy Finerman's her name. She is persistent, diligent, and a wonderful producer. She had an option on the book through Steve Tish's company, and they laid it off at Warner Bros., where Winston Groom, the author of the novel, took a crack at the screenplay. Then there were two others writers—Charlie Peters and Ernest Thompson—over a period of about three years. But, for whatever reasons, it never quite clicked. So it lay fallow six years, I guess.

FROUG: What persistence she had to keep going.

ROTH: Yeah, she really believed in it.

FROUG: And when she came to you, Warner Bros. was still ready to put up more money for you. Right?

ROTH: This wasn't Warner's anymore. She had given the book to Tom and to me to see if we would be interested in being involved in it. Tom said that he would and I said that I would. They were willing to put it in turnaround at Warner Bros., so we went and sold it to Paramount.

FROUG: Warner has been killing themselves ever since. Right?

ROTH: Well, it didn't make 'em happy. I think they'll review their turnaround procedures a little bit, you know.

FROUG: Let me ask you about tackling this job. The story seems almost spineless, it's basically episodic.

ROTH: Definitely episodic.

FROUG: Isn't that difficult for a writer? Obviously you achieved the miracle of making an episodic piece sustain itself throughout the two hours.

ROTH: I think it actually does have a spine. It has perfect bookends, because it has the bus bench, so you have a place and time. The book, to be honest with you, wasn't my cup of tea when I read it, and I didn't really read the whole thing at first. It was a little farcical for me, but I loved the way it traversed history. So I said I'm going to have to throw out what I don't like, and do anything I want. I was thinking about how to tell a story and I remembered Arthur Penn's *Little Big Man*, with him interviewing Dustin Hoffman in the beginning.

FROUG: Hoffman was playing a 121-year-old western pioneer who'd lived with both the Native Americans and the whites.

ROTH: And when you had that sort of blessed premise, you could go anywhere you wanted to. That was the same thing I felt that *Gump* had, too.

FROUG: It did have the same qualities, as a matter of fact.

ROTH: Particularly that device. It wasn't your traditional flashback. You could use narration and go anywhere. If you look at the movie closely, it jumps all over in place and time in an odd way. And I think that the original script did so even more. But it gave me the freedom to do anything I wanted. It was episodic, yet at least somewhere it was grounded. Then you find a love story that kind of follows through the whole piece. I think that's the backbone.

FROUG: That's totally your invention, right?

ROTH: Well, there was a love story in the other one, but it's very, very different.

FROUG: Is it reasonable to say that this narrative device on the bus bench goes back to the primitive fundamental storytelling device of "once upon a time . . ."?

ROTH: Exactly. As a matter of fact, I started to use that but Bob never put it on the screen. Bob thought it was gilding the lily, but the screenplay opens with a line that says a lot of this is true.

FROUG: The same sort of device.

ROTH: Yeah. That's what it was supposed to have said on the screen. The irony was that most of the absurd things were true, the fantasy elements were more a kind of reality. But, you're right, "once upon a time . . ."

FROUG: Since the cavemen, I guess, that's been the device. Sit around the fire and say, "The other night I was walking through the forest . . .", whatever the hell.

ROTH: Exactly.

FROUG: How long did you spend writing it?

ROTH: It took me about eight months, which for me is not that long, really. I'm slow. The one I'm doing now for Coppola has taken over a year.

FROUG: What are you working on now?

ROTH: I'm doing the first thirty years of the CIA.

FROUG: Starting with Wild Bill Donovan?

ROTH: Well, I'm using one character who is a roman à clef, really. He's a guy who was involved in counter intelligence for a number of years. I'm starting actually at Yale in 1938, before the OSS, and then going into the OSS, etc.

FROUG: So there's kind of a Wild Bill character in it.

ROTH: Definitely.

FROUG: That sounds to me like an incredibly difficult job.

ROTH: I think I bit off more than I could chew. [Laughter] That's why I'd rather not go to work this morning.

FROUG: Let me ask you about a film of yours that I just happen to adore, *Memories of Me*. Did your father feel like you were writing about him?

ROTH: Alan King was not playing my father. I had a great uncle who was an extra. I remember going to visit him in this pathetic apartment in Hollywood. His claim to fame was that he played what he called the Talking Violin and was Adolphe Menjou's stand-in, which was his big claim to fame.

FROUG: That's marvelous.

ROTH: The movie is good, but I think it could have been a lot better.

FROUG: Which of your films has been the easiest for you? Has there been an easy one?

ROTH: Um, the easiest. That's a tough question. I guess they all have levels of difficulty. I think the first draft of *Gump* was probably the easiest. The rewriting was maybe harder, but not because the writing was so hard, but just because Zemeckis is very methodical. Every day we'd go back to page one. But not in a negative way. He was always just reexamining. It's his process of working, which I ended up, obviously, respecting. Even before we shot the movie, I respected it. I think we improved things. I used to say, "What the fuck is this guy doing? It's driving me insane." But it was not, as it is with many directors, done because of insecurity. Bob's also a writer. It was his way of knowing the movie better than anybody.

FROUG: And knowing it through the eyes of the writer, moreover.

ROTH: Exactly. In the long run, it was an arduous process, but it was well worth it. Best of all, I liked that he'd tell you in advance the dates when you would be finished. I mean there was no bullshit.

FROUG: That's wonderful. Did you go on the set?

ROTH: Yeah, I was on the set. I went every couple of weeks. I was there for maybe a total of a month.

FROUG: Did Zemeckis let you feel you were part of the actual team?

ROTH: Oh, completely.

FROUG: Did you do any revising as you were shooting?

ROTH: Almost nothing, which is what I love about Bob. We fixed whatever we needed to with rehearsals, and that was pretty much it. That was the movie. The night before he started filming, we talked about the movie and Bob really knew it better than I did at that point.

FROUG: That is a wonderful writer-director relationship.

ROTH: Yeah, and very rare. I wish we could always have that.

FROUG: On *Memories of Me*, Crystal received a co-credit. Did he rewrite you?

ROTH: No, no. Billy and I wrote it together.

FROUG: From scratch?

ROTH: Yeah, from scratch. We sat there like Ferrante and Teicher. We were very close friends and we still are. It was fun. We sort of blended so that Billy became a dramatist and I didn't fear trying comedy.

FROUG: Tell me about your experiences on *Mr. Jones*.

ROTH: *Mr. Jones* was a nightmare. It'd be a great class on how to fuck up what I think was a great piece of material.

FROUG: Tell me the story of *Mr. Jones*.

ROTH: I had had a fairly successful movie at Tristar called *Suspect* with Cher and Dennis Quaid. I had a good relationship with Tristar because the movie had done fairly well, and they thought it was a fairly prestigious project. So they asked me what I wanted to do next, and I said I wanted to do a melodrama, like *Suspicion*, but set around a medical scene. As I started investigating medical mysteries, particularly psychological ones, I discovered manic depression. The script was a very arduous kind of journey, it was a very hard script to write. It was about people facing loss, which, I think, was really the theme of the thing. A very diligent psychiatrist, who was going through certain personal problems, develops a relationship with this anonymous manic depressive, whom she discovers is possibly a genius but won't commit himself to recognize that he's sick. And I thought it was a pretty magnificent script. I really worked hard on it with my wife, who ended up producing the movie. Marty Ritt was gonna do it, and while we were just getting ready to shoot, Marty died of a heart attack.

FROUG: He was the nicest man.

ROTH: He was a wonderful guy and serious filmmaker who dealt with important things. It was an honor to work with him. But now, they brought in a director called Mick Jackson who had done *L.A. Story* and went on to do *The Bodyguard*. He was a nice enough man, but I realized over lunch that he didn't quite get what this was about. We had one other meeting where he sort of gave me a general idea of what he wanted done, and then I floundered trying to figure out what the hell he wanted, and he never would meet with me. I worked on that script for what seems like two or three years, while I was doing other things. It was a very serious piece of work and may be my best piece of just pure, original writing. It was very intricate and I could see the rewrite wasn't really helping it. During every conversation I had with him over the telephone, he generally gave me nonsensical ideas. So I turned it into him, and the studio called up my wife, who was producing, and said, "Your husband's fired." [Laughter] She's sitting at a coffee table across from me. She hangs up and says, "You're fired, honey."

FROUG: [Laughter] What a great story.

ROTH: Yeah. It's an absolutely true story, too, and it really hurt me because this one was totally my flesh and blood. It was a total original, a totally goof-ball idea, totally unique. It wasn't just a melodrama you come up with or a thriller or something. Anyway, they hired another writer who didn't quite get it, and who I thought detracted from what was there. It all became kind of rancorous. Then they brought in a couple of other writers, and eventually the director quit because he never understood the fucking thing anyway. [Laughter] They went on to get another director, who I think is a good director, but I don't think he understood it either. I was never involved after that, except for being brought back at the end to rewrite a couple of scenes.

FROUG: Was your wife still the producer?

ROTH: Yeah, well, we had a big family decision. I said, "Stay with it. You know the integrity of the piece." But it was hopeless. The end product has, as you can see, some of the interesting things in it, but it's a mishmash. They turned at least half of it into sort of a banal love story. It makes no sense. The original script really resonated, I think. Everybody who read it said it's a magnificent piece of work. Anyway, they just killed it, and they spent fortunes killing it.

FROUG: Of course.

ROTH: I mean they kept bringing in very high-priced writers and ended up paying me an ungodly fortune to rewrite one scene toward the end. It was just ridiculous. My wife and I could write a wonderful story about the whole thing, about the profligate waste of money and the people who, even though they may or may not have been talented, never understood what it was about.

FROUG: You still haven't mentioned my favorite word, which is "theme." When you approach something like *Mr. Jones*, you obviously approach it with the theme in mind, and the writing evolves out of your developing interest in the theme.

ROTH: Yes, definitely.

FROUG: Are you able to do that with most of your projects?

ROTH: I think so, at least I try to. I think you have to have a theme. At least I do. I think you need something to always go back to.

"I think you have to have a theme. At least I do. I think you need something to always go back to."

FROUG: Absolutely. I did a script based on the Dalton family and the Coffeyville raid that I sold to your mother thirty years ago. I loved that screenplay and gave it to Walter Newman. Walter said it was a wonderful screenplay. And I said thanks. Then he said, "I just have one question. What's it about?"

ROTH: What's it about, yeah.

FROUG: He destroyed me. [Laughter]

ROTH: It's a tough one.

FROUG: It's the toughest question of all, isn't it?

ROTH: Yeah, that is always the toughest question. Walter was pretty good at doing that kind of stuff. A more honorable man you wouldn't find.

FROUG: That's true, but his question killed me. I was destroyed. And now, thirty years later, I still from time to time ask myself, What was that screenplay about? I mean, I know the story, I know all the events and the characters, but what was it about? What was it saying? I don't know.

ROTH: Exactly. My instinct says that at least fifty percent of the writers know what they're writing about and maybe twenty-five percent of the directors know what they're directing. They take a job and then they try to figure out what it's about rather than figuring it out before they take the job.

FROUG: Why do they bring in writer after writer after writer after writer?

ROTH: My theory is that they get tired of what they bought, and so they figure something fresh will give it a whole new feeling and look and sort of rejuvenate excitement.

FROUG: Looking for magic?

ROTH: Yeah. I think, in some instances, it's probably true that the writer, through this horrible process, just gets tired. I mean, it's very hard to get the juices flowing after a while unless you have a unique director who can give you new areas to have some imagination about. They beat the same scene to death, they're never willing to try it in a whole new, different way and in a new location and everything else. They just take the same scene and location and want the dialogue fixed up. That's never going to change anything. Amusingly, when they ask you to rewrite, they say that they want something totally different, but they also say that they have to have this particular location because they're gonna shoot there in a week and the actors are obviously the same and the story hasn't changed. So you can't have something that comes out of the blue, you can't give them too many miracles.

FROUG: Under the new Writers Guild MBA, apparently they have some sort of restrictions. The original writer gets more shots at the rewrites than he or she used to.

ROTH: That would be great, but I think it's useless unless the director can give some direction. Otherwise, as I say, at some point you need to have some new infusion of blood. It could be the old writer who could do it, but I think you need some new take on it or at least permission to do something new.

FROUG: When you get so that you're the hot writer of the moment, the flavor of the month, which is where you are right now, how do you decide what projects to take on and what not to take on?

ROTH: First of all, you've got to decide what you think you can do best, what's most interesting to you. Before *Gump* even came out, my agent asked me what I wanted to do next, and I said I've always wanted to do this CIA idea. So we took it and searched around to see who would be interested. Francis's [Ford Coppola] company was, and we went to him. Then in the midst of my work on that, Redford sent me a book, *The Horse Whispers*. I wanted to work with him because I think he's an interesting personality, a talented man, and I thought I could do well with this particular piece of material.

FROUG: How many pieces do you work on at the same time?

ROTH: I usually only work on one. The reason these two have dovetailed a little bit is that I'm so far behind on the CIA one. It required such voluminous research, it's been such agony.

FROUG: What kind of time do you allow yourself when you start a screenplay?

ROTH: I think it changes. The CIA one I knew was gonna take me a good year just because of the amount of research. I knew it was going to take a long time to become conversant with it. The one I've just started for Redford I told him I'd have by September. I started, let's say, May 1st or April 15th, so what we're talking about is maybe six months.

FROUG: Along with the CIA story, that's a heavy schedule.

ROTH: Yeah, but I'm just about done with the CIA, and the other one is very well laid out—the book is very straightforward, so it's a different kind of writing.

FROUG: When you're writing for Coppola, is he in on the writing?

ROTH: No, not really. We sort of made an agreement: I'd write; he'd wait to read. Fair enough?

FROUG: Being the flavor of the month, how do you get out from under the stresses and strains, which are sitting out in front of you all the time, and get to be with yourself?

ROTH: Well, I really don't think I've changed that way at all. I sort of live for my family. I love my kids and enjoy that. And I've been around long enough to know I'm the flavor of the month. In a sense, the Oscar gives you the one thing they can't quite take away from you: everybody knows my contribution, and I feel great about that. So I think I've worked my way up to the money. It's not like I sold a script and all of a sudden they're paying me that. I think, after the years I've put in, I have certain abilities and I've gotten better at certain things. So I think that I've earned it, if anyone deserves that kind of ridiculous money.

FROUG: How long have you been writing?

ROTH: I've been writing since about 1970—twenty-five-odd years.

FROUG: When did you decide that screenwriting was what you wanted to do in life? Being the offspring of top Hollywood professionals, were you born a writer?

ROTH: I guess I obviously got something through them. I think my mother's got a great eye for detail and recreating and writing about it. And I think that's one of my strong suits. I guess they gave me their love for movies; I do love movies and I'm not afraid of the business, which I think is good.

FROUG: When did you write your first script?

"I do love movies and I'm not afraid of the business, which I think is good."

ROTH: I guess I wrote my first script, *Harmonica Patriot*, in 1970. It won the Samuel Goldwyn Screenwriting Writing Award at UCLA.

FROUG: *Fifty/Fifty* is the best student screenplay I've ever read. An outstanding piece of work of the highest professional level. The theme was so powerful and it was so powerfully written. I was approaching age fifty when I read it, and I really related to it. And now you can relate to it.

ROTH: Yeah, now I can relate to it. It's lovely. [Laughter]

FROUG: You've got a great life, and you seem to be enjoying every bit of it. Are you working on another original?

ROTH: Well, this CIA one is an original, definitely an original. I don't know what I'm going to do next. I like to be as different as possible. I've been talking to Spielberg about something that's totally different than these two, so that's kind of exciting.

FROUG: An idea he threw at you?

ROTH: Yeah. I'm not quite sure how to dramatize it yet, but it would be so totally different. The greatest thing about writing is that you get to enter a whole world where you've never been before. I don't know how these guys who write nothing but thrillers or action pictures or whatever keep on doing it. I admire the work they do, but I don't know how they do it time and time again. In other words, to me, it just seems like a job.

FROUG: Well, I couldn't agree more, because I did it.

ROTH: Yeah, you know what I'm saying. I could never write television, not because it's not a craft, but because it's writing the same thing every week. I guess you find ways to be creative within that.

"The greatest thing about writing is that you get to enter a whole world where you've never been before."

FROUG: Yes, you do, but it's narrow and you do feel like you're in a kind of closet. That's why I became a teacher.

ROTH: I say to myself, Gee, what's another great new world I can explore? It's wonderful. I feel so lucky.

FROUG: With that marvelous enthusiasm you've always had for the track, why haven't you done a track movie?

ROTH: The only one that was even semi-successful was the Kubrick one, *The Killing*, which was about the knock-off of a race track. I tried one years ago called *The Dream Team*, which was about a jockey. It was from a book by Joe McGuiness. A jockey, a woman reporter, and an old-time gambler go to Hialeah on a scam. It didn't work.

FROUG: Does your wife share your enthusiasm for the track?

ROTH: I like to gamble on the horses, but I also just enjoy the day out there. I have friends, and we see each other every day we're out there. I enjoy their lives and their own ways. They're desperate people, but they're interesting. And it's a place where they couldn't give a shit what I do for a living. In other words, it's a totally different world.

FROUG: Do you think maybe that's where you release the pressure cooker you live with in the movie industry?

ROTH: Yeah, definitely.

FROUG: You get over there and it's a world where nobody gives a shit who you are or what you do and you're out from under the twenty-four-hour-a-day pressure you must get from agents, producers, and, most of all, the screenplay you're working on. right?

ROTH: No doubt about it. But I really don't have much to do with producers or agents. I mean, I like my agent, but I'm still nasty. Otherwise they'll just kill you. I got my kids; I got my family. I make a nice living, but if they take that away, they do. You know what I'm saying? So I still say "fuck you" all the time. Otherwise they'll just use you.

CREDITS

Forrest Gump, 1994 (Oscar winner, based on the novel by Winston Groom)

Jane's House, 1992 (CBS M.O.W.)

The Heights, 1993, FOX-TV

Mr. Jones, 1992 (shared credit)

Memories of Me, 1987 (co-written with Billy Crystal)

Suspect, 1987 (sole credit)

Nickel Ride, 1973 (sole credit)

Uncredited Participating Writing On:

The Drowning Pool, 1976

The Onion Field, 1979

Wolfen, 1981

Rhapsody in August, 1991

Apollo 13, 1995

*Show me a congenital eavesdropper with the instincts of a
Peeping Tom and I will show you the makings of a dramatist.*
—Kenneth Tynan, *Pausing on the Stairs*

Cynics have claimed there are only six basic plots.
Frankenstein *and* My Fair Lady *are really the same story.*
—Leslie Halliwell, *The Filmgoer's Book of Quotes*

*The thriller is the extension of the fairy tale. It is melodrama so
embellished as to create the illusion that the story being told,
however unlikely, could be true.*
—Raymond Chandler, *Raymond Chandler Speaking*

You Gotta Have It

In *Screenwriting Tricks of the Trade*, I remarked that good screenplays have a lot in common with classical music. I was surprised and delighted to find confirmation of this in A. Alvarez's recent *New Yorker* article about the renowned pianist Alfred Brendel.

In his lengthy piece, A. Alvarez writes, "One of the most important lessons Brendel taught Imogen Cooper was that there is a tension that goes all the way through a piece of music and never lets up. 'He used to talk about the long silver cord that one pulls on,' she said. 'He'd crouch down beside the piano and say, "Go on, pull, pull."

Sometimes there's a little kink in the cord, but it never sags. There's always a force irresistibly pulling it from the first note to the last. He used to say, "You've got to get the audience from the first note." I'd say you've got to get the audience from the moment you come through the door.'"

I can not imagine a more important foundation for a great screenplay than Mr. Brendel's "silver cord." Whether you describe your line of action as a silver cord or any other metaphor is your personal choice. The essential fact is that if you want to write a great screenplay, you've got to find a *single action line* in your story that will hold your audience from page one until FADE OUT.

What Will Happen Next?

Aristotle, the greatest teacher of stage drama in recorded history, said more than two thousand years ago, "Among simple plots and actions the episodic are the worst. By 'episodic' I mean one in which there is no probability or necessity for the order in which the episodes follow one another. Such structures are composed by the bad poets."

What worked on the stages of ancient Greece often still works on our stages and in our films. Yet on the subject of episodic storytelling, Ari was dead wrong. But then the master didn't have movies in mind.

I urge you to consider the episodic form before beginning your screenplay. It can make old stories seem fresh and new. Most important of all, episodic storytelling usually guarantees surprises, whereas cause-and-effect storytelling has a certain built-in predictability factor that can be difficult to overcome—you start out with an added burden: How will I generate surprise for my audience? You can eliminate that problem by telling your story in episodic style.

Surprise remains one of the screenwriter's strongest storytelling devices. I cannot stress this point too strongly.

In view of the successful history of episodic films, both high- and low-budget, it's surprising how few screenwriters are tapping into this storytelling device, which has been used since the dawn of time and the dawn of movies (D.W. Griffith's *The Birth of a Nation*, for instance).

Movies based on episodic screenplays often walk off with Oscars, garner impressive reviews, and instigate lines at the box office. And they often serve as excellent calling cards for young filmmakers. Consider recent low-budget films that launched new careers at the Sundance Film Festival: *Clerks* and *Smoke*. Both of these episodic films are anchored by the *unity of place*—the former by a cigar store, the latter by a small convenience and video-rental store. (What makes them even more noteworthy is that both were made on budgets less than the price of a Hollywood star's wardrobe.)

Consider these examples of highly successful episodic screenplays that were made into big-hit, big award-winning movies:

Forrest Gump was written for the screen by Eric Roth, based on Winston Groom's novel. Gump sits on a bus-stop bench and tells us episodes from his life. Each episode is not necessarily connected to the next. Sometimes they seem random, but when needed, they cut back to Gump on his bench, where he continues his narration (Voice Over), describing a new episode that leaps to another time and place. The bench (unity of place) anchored the story. Of course, that is not the only reason that this particular episodic movie worked so well, won Eric Roth an Oscar, and reached over 350 million dollars in box-office receipts. The most important reason was that *audiences the world over were fascinated with the central character and his unusual situation.* How does a young man with a seventy-five IQ meet the challenges of getting through life's rigors in the difficult and complex world we live in? That was the emotional spine of the story, upon which Eric could hang episode after episode without fear of losing his audience. The line of action, in this instance, was also the theme of the movie.

The value of the audience not knowing what's going to happen next cannot be overstated, *provided the film is centered on characters who are sufficiently fascinating.* When the audience is fascinated by your protagonist(s) and cannot predict what will happen to him or her next, you've got them hooked. And, even more importantly, you've got producers, directors, actors, agents, studio readers, et al. hooked. Long before your movie is shown to an audience, you have to hook scores of readers.

The key here, as it is in so many outstanding episodic movies, is an utterly fascinating character who doesn't ask for our attention; he or she grabs it. *Write a movie about a nothing-will-stand-in-my-way, fascinating character overcoming obstacle after obstacle and the chances are that your audience will be hooked.*

Consider the episodic film *Driving Miss Daisy.* This story of an elderly Southern Jewish lady begins with her having a minor car accident caused because her age has robbed her of the ability to drive safely. Her son, over her vehement protests, hires a chauffeur to drive her, but this strong, exceedingly stubborn lady will not let anybody rob her of her independence. The theme and the line of action in this are identical. They are best summed up by Dylan

Thomas's poem to his father, "Do not go gentle into that good night, rage, rage, against the dying of the light."

From the first minutes of the film, we see a strong-willed, determined woman who will fight for independence until finally and inevitably she has to be put in a nursing home. Here again is the nothing-will-stand-in-my-way character determined to live her life as she sees fit. Screenwriter Alfred Uhry (working from his own play) immediately establishes the obstacle his protagonist must try to overcome—encroaching old age.

You must always remember that no drama can hold an audience, or even a reader, without confronting the protagonist(s) with major obstacles as quickly and as often as possible. These obstacles are what generate conflict; they should keep escalating throughout your story. Just like in life, something often goes wrong. How you deal with these obstacles determines whether your screenplay will be a drama, a melodrama, a comedy, a tragicomedy, or a farce. The attitude of the principal character(s) toward what goes wrong will almost always create the conflict.

Another outstanding example of the viability of episodic drama is the classic World War II film *Patton*, winner of Best Picture and

Best Screenplay Oscars (episodic films have a habit of winning both Oscars and audiences). Here we have a powerful, brilliant, fanatical general who is so driven to win the war on his own terms that he persists in defying the orders of his superiors. He is the epitome of the nothing-will-stand-in-my-way character. His bullheadedness is also his undoing. The obstacle that he cannot overcome is himself. Francis Ford Coppola and Edmund North's screenplay is a masterpiece of episodic drama.

The same applies to stories with multiple major characters. An outstanding example is *Steel Magnolias* by Robert Harling, based on his play. This comedy about six small-town Southern women is held together by both a unity of place (the local beauty parlor) and a unity of theme (the leading characters' determination to overcome their lives' difficulties). As you study this film, note that every scene is centered on conflict, albeit played comedicly.

As with many movies, this film's theme is stated plainly toward the end by one of the major characters: "Life goes on." These steel magnolias are each, in her own way, powerful women who will let nothing stand in their way. This episodic movie is a lesson in the absolute need for conflict in every scene and an outstanding example of how to write multiple-protagonist drama-comedy.

Does the episodic form work only in drama? No, it works in any genre. Consider the 1970 movie *M★A★S★H*, surely among the top ten comedies of all time. Ring Lardner, Jr., won an Oscar for his screenplay, which was completely episodic—a series of frantic, wildly funny adventures of surgeons at a Mobile Army Surgical Hospital during the Korean War. Here and there are threads that connect scenes and become sequences: the arrival of Chief Nurse Houlihan ("Hot Lips"), the rigid disciplinarian; the frantic sexual coupling of Hot Lips and Frank Burns, the holier-than-thou, self-righteous doctor, that is broadcast to the entire encampment. Hilarious sequence follows hilarious sequence. But it is centered in a single location (unity of place): the Mobile Army Surgical Hospital. The action line and the theme are the same—wild, unbridled humor is the antidote for the insanity of war.

M★A★S★H is strung together loosely, moving from unrelated sequence to unrelated sequence. Cause and effect are only rarely of consequence. The football game has nothing whatever to do with the dentist's suicide attempt, nor does it connect in any way to the passionate affair of Hot Lips and Frank Burns. The best way to describe the structure of this hilarious romp is that funny stuff happens. It follows the fundamental rule of all comedy: keep it funny and keep it fast.

M*A*S*H is held together by the three Aristotelian unities: the unity of time, place, and theme. It is essential in episodic stories that there be a strong, unifying force. Whether you have all three of these unifying elements or not, you must have at least one unifying element upon which to hang disconnected sequences. (Having all three is the best insurance that an episodic screenplay will be a winner.)

Episodic storytelling will not rise to greatness nor broad audience acceptance without a strong, unifying action line and/or theme that runs through the film like a flexible steel cable from which all sorts of events (scenes) can hang as jewels from a bracelet.

Rising Action and the Corkscrew

During my years of teaching screenwriting, I would often draw a schematic of the classic three-act structure (the most common but by no means the only form used by most dramatists). As I diagrammed the approximate length of each act, I would draw a single, upwardly slanted line through the graph. This is the line of Rising Action.

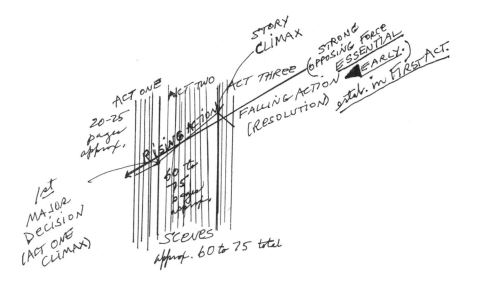

An in-depth explanation of the elements shown in this diagram can be found in my *Scrrenwriting Tricks of the Trade,* published by Silman-James Press.

Your action line should never be horizontal. If it is, your drama will be static. Lajos Egri tells us that drama is built on *rising* action, *escalating* dramatic tension, and conflict—the difficulties *increase* until the story reaches its climax.

It is vital to your story that excitement increases as the story moves along. If you allow your story to become horizontal it will go flat, and your audience (or reader) will doze off. Causes-and-effects plots demand that each sequence force the next sequence, and so on, holding your story firmly linked (literally a chain of events), driving upward toward its climax.

Do not be misled into believing that episodic drama or comedy is non-linear. In spite of the sometimes seemingly random placement of scenes, *there is always a strong line to hang them on*, whether it is a line of action or a strong, unifying theme (or both). Truly non-linear stories (as opposed to episodic stories) are inevitably a disaster (with the arguable exception of Fellini's *8 1/2* and *Juliet of the Spirits*, neither of which helped save the Italian cinema from going belly up).

Note that most episodic screenplays are character-driven as opposed to plot-driven. Character-driven stories might be said to be shaped like a corkscrew, with the writer driving the conflict down, around, and deep into the heart and soul of the protagonist. The pressure here is on the writer to uncork the innermost turmoil and fears of the protagonist. Herein lie the surprises. Each scene should dramatize a new and fascinating aspect of the protagonist, which will be revealed by conflict. Your audience receives a special bonus when your protagonist's new revelation is paradoxical, unexpected, seemingly "out of character."

We cannot leave the subject of episodic screenplays without mentioning the grand master of all episodic dramas: *Citizen Kane*. The scenes of this episodic drama are not only non-sequential, they cut back and forth in time and place with abandon. The action line that holds this seemingly structureless film together is a detective story—two reporters trying to unearth the mystery of Charles Foster Kane's dying word, "Rosebud." The drive to unearth the meaning of this word allows us to be whipped from phase to phase of Kane's life as remembered by his surviving friends, with no regard for sequencing or causes and effects. Orson Welles and Herman Mankiewicz won Oscars for their screenplay. (Do you notice a pattern here for writers of episodic screenplays?)

Kane is the best single argument for episodic film drama. I urge you to consider this frequently awarded and rewarding form of storytelling as you approach your next screenplay. You could surprise yourself.

· · · · ·

Find a strong-willed character with a nothing-will-stand-in-my-way determination to reach his or her goal confronting strong opposition, add a strong action line, keep throwing obstacles (conflicts) in his or her path, and you're well on your way to a gripping screenplay. The chances are that the right structure will unfold as you write. Your character(s)—with his, her, or their drive to achieve a goal—will propel you forward. If they do not, you have not given them tough enough obstacles or conflicts. In drama, as in life, nothing worth achieving comes easily.

Making your characters meet challenges full force is what drama is all about. As you get inside your characters, you will know them intimately and they will become so real that they will speak their dialogue to you. This is one of the true joys of writing.

Since art is a trial-and-error process, free yourself to be your most creative. Pull out all the stops; writing drama is not for wimps. When you invest your characters with dynamic energy your screenplay will come alive.

I still wonder what certain characters in some of my screenplays are doing now, how their life is going. They still live in my mind. I wonder what will happen to them next.

Rewrite is Might

It is axiomatic that writing is rewriting, especially screenwriting. It is an unavoidable part of your job.

For many years, UCLA graduate screenwriting students asked the writing faculty to offer a course in rewriting. We always refused because we preferred to start our students on new material, following through from concept to a final polished draft. Furthermore, every rewrite brings with it its own unique problems not necessarily applicable to any other script. There are no rules for rewriting, only the recognition that it is a critical function of screenwriting.

However, here are some suggestions for your consideration as you approach this phase of your screenplay:

After you've written FADE OUT on your first draft, put your screenplay aside for at least a day or two, preferably a longer period of time. Meanwhile, engage in an activity that is as far away from your screenplay-thinking as possible: (a) go to the gym and work out, (b) take a trip, (c) have sex, (d) clean the house, do anything that will cleanse your mind of the screenplay on which you've been working. I call this the "cooling off" period. Its purpose is to allow you to come back to the screenplay with as much objectivity as possible. You want to reread your first draft with fresh eyes, as though you were not the author of it.

Now, and only now, can you approach the rewriting with a certain dispassion. (As I mentioned in *Screenwriting Tricks of the Trade*, never, never start rewriting your screenplay while you are writing it. That is the certain road to a never-completed screenplay. As you are moving along with your draft-in-progress—first, second, third draft, ad infinitum—make notes in the margins about ideas you have for rewriting *after you've finished the draft*.)

As you reread your draft, ask yourself the following questions:

How close is this to what I set out to do?

Did I tell my story with clarity and purpose?

Did I lose myself in a torrent of words?

Have I lost my action line along the way?

Is the script an honest expression of my theme?

Is it an easy read for the people to whom I want to send it?

Have I hooked the reader by page ten?

Is the screenplay over-written?

Am I verbose—do I use ten words when one will do?

Am I trying to direct the film as well as write the screenplay?

When you rewrite, you first must focus on the big picture, the overview of the work. Don't get lost in the minutiae, which is tempting because small errors are so easy to fix. In musicians' terms, don't focus on the notes, focus on the shape and sound of the symphony as a whole. And *when in doubt, cut it out.*

Some writers get caught up in endless rewriting while striving for perfection. Some famous screenwriters get so locked into the process that they cannot let their scripts go. They become trapped in a nightmare of endless rewriting. It's not difficult to allow yourself to become confused and bewildered in a sea of changes. Stop yourself before you reach this dangerous point. Falling in love with your own words is a serious problem, but getting lost in them is worse.

Keep in mind that there is no such thing as the "perfect" screenplay. Your job is to make your script as excellent as you can, and then let it go, send it out to agents, producers, studios, actors, et al., and hope for the best.

If you discover during your objective analysis of your nth rewrite that it is still not working for you, even though you've trimmed it to the bone, there's one final step you can take. Break down your screenplay onto lined scene cards, one 4x6 card per scene, lay out your scenes on a flat surface, and re-examine your structure. Perhaps that's where your problem lies; you haven't structured your story well. This, I suggest, is a test of last resort. Ask yourself if you've begun your screenplay at the point of attack—that point in a story that nothing need come before but something must follow. When you have a problem with the beginning of your screenplay, often it is because you haven't started your story within the first ten pages. You've become preoccupied with "setting it up." "Setting up" your situation should be accomplished in the first scene—within three or four pages at most—while you simultaneously get your story underway.

Getting underway immediately is critical. Your reader will give you a maximum of ten pages to hook him or her. If you haven't, you're immediately placed in the large stack of rejects. Hook 'em fast, hook 'em quick, preferably on page one.

Screenwriting, like all art, is trial and error. There is no sure or certain way to proceed, no guarantee that you will "get it right." You will probably write several screenplays before you begin to get the feel for it. However, if you're serious about your work, you will suffer through the growing pains, the process of teaching yourself what works for you and what doesn't. Every screenwriter who ever lived began by struggling through that difficult first screenplay, and then rewriting it and rewriting it until, finally, he or she could look at that 120-page polished draft and proudly say, "I did it, and I finally got it right." On more than one occasion in my life I've been convinced that my script did not come to life until after my first major rewrite.

(Rewriting became so prevalent a demand by producers, actors, directors, etc., that some years ago the Writers Guild of America won a contractual limit of two rewrites and a polish. Newcomers are often slow to understand that the WGA is the screenwriter's salvation. I am most proud to have been designated a Lifetime Member by the WGA's Board of Directors.)

The principal aim of all storytelling is to expose the inner working of the human mind through conflict, whether it be told in a short story, novel, radio, movie, or play.
—Lajos Egri, *The Art of Dramatic Writing*

Why shouldn't truth be stranger than fiction? Fiction, after all, has to make sense.
—Mark Twain

I have tried to remove weight, sometimes from people, sometimes from heavenly bodies, sometimes from cities; above all I have tried to remove weight from the structure of stories and from language.
—Italo Calvino, *Six Memos for the Next Millennium*

Peoples Who Need Peoples

An Interview with

David and Janet Peoples

"Raymond Chandler says that you have to have passion: technique alone is just an embroidered potholder. I do think that what a screenwriter is doing is expressing feelings in a screenplay. Or, at least, that's part of what a screenwriter is doing. After all, it's an entertainment business, you're trying to entertain people. So you've got those two things—the desire to entertain people and the desire to express your feelings. You try and mix them so they work." —David Peoples

"If you write a screenplay by yourself, you think that everything's there, even though you know that you might not have accomplished everything that you set out to do. And when you finish it, you're amazed and horrified that in four or five places you have changed scenes and that there are holes—people couldn't understand main story points—and you have to reel back from this and start correcting it. You may, in fact, get a suggestion from somebody that takes you a whole different way. When you collaborate, you get that from your partner all the way through. You're not waiting for the very end. You're hammering and hammering and hammering and saying, "I don't understand" or "do you know why you did this?" or "what was the motivation?" or "what's your intention here?" You critique each other's work. At the same time, you try to preserve the best and move forward with the best." —Janet Peoples

David Webb Peoples certainly did not invent the Western, which has arguably been America's favorite movie genre since the *first* American movie, *The Great Train Robbery* in 1903. For nine decades, audiences have watched good guys in white hats fight bad guys in black hats, as heroic sheriffs tamed wild, drunken, Godless towns, during carefully choreographed shoot-outs. Villains were unmistakable and were always punished for their sins. Our traditional Westerns were comfortable, unchallenging, mostly mindless entertainment for the whole family. Not surprisingly, audiences all over the world loved them, too. One of the most reliable aspects of the American Western is that you always knew the good guy would win in a mano-à-mano showdown with the bad guy. Good Always Triumphed Over Evil. This inspiring message was imposed by the motion-picture industry's own censorship code, and also by the studio tsars who were steadfast in their determination to send the customers out of the theater with happy smiles on their faces.

Gradually, the moguls died off, as did the Hays Office, the Johnson office, etc., along with the rigidity of their Hollywood notion of approved morality.

In 1964, the Italian writer-director Sergio Leone came along and invented the "spaghetti Western"—a dark, violent exercise in the triumph of evil—and in the process, made Clint Eastwood the world's top box-office draw. Leone made a series of these genre movies, culminating in 1969 with his epic-length, magnificently photographed *Once Upon a Time in the West*.

And then, in the '80s, along came screenwriter David Webb Peoples, who took the American Western and turned its conventions upside down and inside out with his original screenplay *Unforgiven*.

You could no longer tell the good guys from the bad guys—everybody embodied elements of both good and evil (just like in real, as opposed to reel, life). The sheriff, brilliantly played by Gene Hackman, was as enigmatic and ambiguous as everybody else. The protagonist was an alcoholic, sociopathic pig farmer who killed as effortlessly as swatting flies and, in the end, after murdering six or eight men, blithely rode off into the sunset, unrepentant, unpunished, and unpursued. We are told by the narrator that William Munny (Eastwood) took his two kids to San Francisco, where he became a successful merchant.

Unforgiven won Oscars for Best Picture (Eastwood as producer), Best Director (Eastwood), and Best Supporting Actor (Gene Hackman): all the major players except (what else is new?) the writer who created everything seen on the screen—all the characters, all the dialogue, the story, the theme, and, actually, the film—in the privacy of his own mind.

• • • • •

In the history of the movies, there have been several outstanding husband-and-wife screenwriting collaborators. Two of the most successful are Irving Ravetch and Harriet Frank, Jr., with a string of most impressive films to their credit (including *Murphy's Romance*, *Norma Rae*, *Conrack*, *Hombre*, and *Hud*). Earlier husband-and-wife screenwriting teams included Henry and Phoebe Ephron (*Desk Set* and *Take Her, She's Mine*).

In recent years, more and more married couples are becoming successful screenwriting teams. Among the outstanding examples are

Bonnie and Terry Turner (*Wayne's World*), Gregory Nava and Anna Thomas (*El Norte*), Nicholas Kazan and Robin Secord (*Matilda*), Nancy Meyers and Charles Shyer (*Father of the Bride*), Lee and Janet Batchler (*Batman Forever*), and David and Janet Peoples (*Twelve Monkeys*). The story of Dave and Janet's collaboration is told on the pages that follow.

"There are really three writers under this roof: There's Janet Peoples, who's written a lot of screenplays; there's David Peoples, who's written a lot of screenplays; and then there's the team—David and Janet Peoples—who have written a lot of screenplays."

FROUG: Now that you've written *Unforgiven*, an Oscar-nominated screenplay and an Oscar-winning movie, you must be a hot property. Do people send you scripts thinking you can fix them?

D. PEOPLES: There's some of that, but Jan and I have been so busy. We're writing together these days.

FROUG: You and your wife?

D. PEOPLES: Yeah. Janet Peoples. She's been a screenwriter for years, and we collaborated on some documentaries a long time ago. In fact, along with Jon Else, we did *The Day After Trinity*, an Oscar-nominated documentary.

FROUG: It's an outstanding piece of work.

D. PEOPLES: Well, we're very proud of it. At any rate, we've also been collaborating on some feature projects recently. There are really three writers under this roof: There's Janet Peoples, who's written a lot of screenplays; there's David Peoples, who's written a lot of screenplays; and then there's the team—David and Janet Peoples—who have written a lot of screenplays.

FROUG: I think we're missing one of the writers.

D. PEOPLES: You want me to get her?

FROUG: Yeah. But before you do, let me ask you one question. Was she your writing partner on *Unforgiven*?

D. PEOPLES: No.

FROUG: Let's discuss that movie first and then we'll talk about the team. *Unforgiven* won Oscars for Best Picture, Best Director, and Best Supporting Actor. Isn't it odd that that film can win all those awards and not win for the screenplay?

D. PEOPLES: I don't know that it's odd. After all, Bruce Beresford got Best Picture for *Driving Miss Daisy* but I don't even remember if he was nominated for Best Director. I don't think you can make sense out of any of it. The screenplay that did win Best Screenplay was a terrific one—*The Crying Game* by Neil Jordan. He did a brilliant job. The Writers Guild voted for the Neil Jordan script as well.

FROUG: I must be a lone voice of dissent. I don't think it was in the same league as *Unforgiven*.

D. PEOPLES: I think you're selling *The Crying Game* short. Jordan did something quite extraordinary. He took characters whom nobody could have made popular or made people want to see, and he made you want to see them and made you care about them. That's a huge accomplishment. As a screenwriter, I think that that's one of the most difficult things to accomplish. Look at what Paul Schrader did with Travis Bickle in *Taxi Driver*. Audiences all over America were not waiting to see some guy like Travis Bickle on the screen, and yet, with Paul Schrader writing it, somehow they did. That's one of the extraordinary things about *The Crying Game*: Jordan took

"I resolved not to have people get killed in my screen- plays. I felt killing was so trivialized in most movies. I didn't think it was a subject to be dealt with in the entertainment industry."

characters that a broad section of the public did not want to go see and, by gosh, we all wanted to see them. It was terrific, and we cared about them. And that's screenwriting.

FROUG: I would not like to hang around with most of the characters in *Unforgiven*. You did exactly the same thing with your characters.

D. PEOPLES: Right. I'm not going to knock *Unforgiven*, it's a great movie. All I'm saying is that *The Crying Game* is quite a script.

FROUG: What motivated you to write such a dark Western?

D. PEOPLES: Well, actually, *Taxi Driver* had a lot to do with it. When I first started to write screenplays, I resolved not to have people get killed in my screenplays. I felt killing was so trivialized in most movies. I didn't think it was a subject to be dealt with in the entertainment industry. When I saw *Taxi Driver*, I had a major change of view. I thought it was an incredible movie, and I thought it didn't trivialize anything. It was respectful to life and to the characters. It was an over- whelmingly powerful and wonderful movie. I think it was a real big thing for a lot of people. We all owe Paul Schrader and Martin Scorsese a lot. Another big thing for me was the wonderful book by Glendon Swarthout called *The Shootist*, which was made into a movie with a script by his son. The movie was good, but it was like a valentine. It was a chance to put an aging Jimmy Stewart with an aging John Wayne and Lauren Bacall, with Ron Howard playing the young boy. It was a sweet movie, a nice movie, but it wasn't *The Shootist*, which was a dark, frightening, powerful, brilliant book. And in the book, the part played by Ron Howard wasn't some cute, nice kid—this guy was going to be a nightmare. The book really excited me and gave me energy. It probably influenced *Unforgiven* a great deal.

FROUG: I thought *Unforgiven* was in many ways a breakthrough movie because all the characters were so ambiguous. When you set out to write it, did you start with the idea of this pig farmer as a recovering alcoholic who had been a former gunslinger and killer? Was that the germ of the character that led you to the story?

D. PEOPLES: Well, actually, the germ was reading *The Shootist*. That inspired me. My first idea was of a gunfighter who was very sick and afraid that he was dying. That was the first scene I had. That was the important scene to get me into writing the movie. I felt that it was the scene that nobody had ever seen: the idea of this human being who's afraid of death, who's not some courageous super hero. That's where I was working from, and as the script began to develop and I began to deal with it, that scene became less and less important. Finally, it became the scene after William Munny is beaten up and is lying up in the cabin, afraid that he's going to die. So that scene stayed in the movie but it ceased to be the main point of the movie. But a lot of the story came from the idea of that man facing death, not being shot or something, but facing death from a fever or whatever and having all those fears and having lived that life.

FROUG: In writing the sheriff, did you have any particular historical sheriff in mind or did you start with this paradoxical, ambiguous sheriff who was both a son of a bitch and an upholder of whatever law and order there was around there?

D. PEOPLES: Well, this was one of the few times I actually was conscious of any thematic material, and it was not so much a conscious theme as it was my way of trying to find an approach to the material. As I said, I never wanted anybody killed in the screenplay because I thought that killing is so trivialized in movies. I don't think killing people is funny. It's not necessarily unnatural, but I do think it's heavy stuff. As I was writing, I decided that these characters in the story were going to kill people for totally different reasons—everybody was in it for a different thing.

FROUG: Can you mention examples?

D. PEOPLES: William Munny killed people because he was almost sociopathic: it just wasn't as hard for him to do it as it was for other people. In some way, I had Travis Bickle in mind. As a young man, Munny could have been a bit like Travis Bickle— somebody out on the street who somehow just doesn't have the same governor on his motor as you or I do. And then there was the kid who thought that killing people was like in the movies. They didn't have movies in those days, but that's the way he thought: He romanticized killing. Subsequently, I saw the sheriff, Little Bill, as the embodiment of rational killing, which is what law enforcement is—trying to do the lesser of two evils. In fact, I'm very sympathetic to Little Bill's position in the movie. He behaved very much like policemen behave. Their job is to minimize violence. In the case of Little Bill, he set out to intimidate everybody so that nobody would get shot. And when he's faced with a bunch of assassins who are coming to town, he publicly whips somebody in order to send out the message that he's not going to tolerate that stuff here, which is not uncharacteristic of the way police behave today, even though the rules are slightly different. In fact, if you watch the cop shows, you see police officers trying to intimidate people. From a liberal point of view, you can be upset that they are abusing the rights of people and that they're misbehaving, but you can also see that at least the intention is to have less violence rather than more violence. It's not right and it's not wrong. It's a continuing problem. When are you abusing? When are you making things better? It's an old story and I was very sympathetic to Little Bill in the sense that he thought that what he was doing was the right thing. He sure got in trouble because he wasn't a feminist. But he didn't have the context in which he could be a good feminist. By the same token, the women had no opportunity to simply act in a powerful way. So there wasn't a right or wrong answer to it. All of these problems are dilemmas that we all face in life. And the final character is English Bob, who was the last to be invented. English Bob kills people for money, he doesn't kill people for some idea of social good, so he is, again, another perspective on this. He did it for cash. Period.

FROUG: Do you believe the screenwriter is obliged to be politically correct? For example, what about Little Bill's mistreatment of women?

D. PEOPLES: A screenwriter has the same obligation as everybody else, which is to try to be a decent person, have a decent point of view.

FROUG: Personally as well as in his or her work?

D. PEOPLES: Yes. Your work either reflects respect and caring for the rest of humanity or it reflects your baser feelings. As a writer, you have an obligation to write, and you want to think that what you're doing is the right thing. Maybe it's not. You can't be the judge of it yourself, but you can try to write the right thing.

FROUG: *Unforgiven* has so much ambiguity in it that a lot of people find it difficult to accept. I showed it at a film class in Hawaii and some people said, "I don't like that movie. It's too violent."

D. PEOPLES: Well, there is violence. Certainly the slashing of Delilah in the opening is violent.

FROUG: Your original title was *The Cut Whore Killings*, wasn't it?

D. PEOPLES: Yes. I watched the movie and said, "Oh God, that's violent." Down the road, the killing of Young Davey is meant to be brutally violent when they sit up in the rocks, just shooting and waiting for him to bleed to death. That's just violent. The movie is violent.

FROUG: A couple of my older students were deeply offended by it.

D. PEOPLES: But I don't think it trivializes violence. Some people have an easier time with trivialized violence than with non-trivialized violence, which I'm not going to argue about. You feel how you feel. You see James Bond and it's all so . . .

FROUG: It's comic violence . . .

D. PEOPLES: The deaths are all so frivolous that you don't get upset about them.

"Your work either reflects respect and caring for the rest of humanity or it reflects your baser feelings."

FROUG: It's mayhem as comedy.

D. PEOPLES: Something like that. I like James Bond movies. They're very entertaining and I'm not a prude about that stuff except when people get on their high horse, get distressed, and call something violent when it's not trivializing violence. I mean, *Taxi Driver* is horrifying in its violence, and it's intended to be horrifying. Violence is horrifying. If you've been around somebody who's being punched, you hear fists hit real-life flesh, which is a sickening sound.

FROUG: What do you think makes a great screenplay or a great screenwriter? What qualities would you deem most important?

D. PEOPLES: Well, you know, I was looking at the old Raymond Chandler biography yesterday, which contains some of his writing about screenwriting. He says that you have to have passion: Technique alone is just an embroidered potholder. I do think that what a screenwriter is doing is expressing feelings in a screenplay. Or, at least, that's part of what a screenwriter is doing. After all, it's an entertainment business, you're trying to entertain people. So you've got two things: The desire to entertain people and the desire to express your feelings. You try and mix them so they work. I think that's what screenwriters do.

FROUG: What was the core idea that launched your screenplay for *Hero*?

D. PEOPLES: Laura Ziskin and Alvin Sargent came to me with an idea about a not-very-appealing fellow who became a national hero by accident. I said, "I don't want to talk with

"Violence is horrifying. If you've been around somebody who's being punched, you hear fists hit real-life flesh, which is a sickening sound."

[163]

you about it because I have a similar idea of my own." I had an idea, which was very dark and very ironic, as my things tend to be, about an extremely unsympathetic guy who saves a whole bunch of people in a fire. Anyway, I said, "Don't tell me about yours." And about a year later, Laura approached me again and we talked a little about it. They had a treatment, and there were things in it that were really terrific, but I wasn't comfortable with it. I just didn't want it to be too lighthearted and cheerful. They were very comfortable with me doing some stuff differently, so I went to work on *Hero* for Laura. I did several drafts and then Stephen Frears came on, and we did some more changes and so on.

FROUG: Ultimately, were you happy with it?

D. PEOPLES: Oh, yes, very happy with it. Absolutely.

FROUG: I've been listening to the woes that my good friend Laurence Dworet had with Dustin Hoffman on *Outbreak*: rewriting the script and bringing in his own writer for his own scenes and so on. Did you have those problems on *Hero*?

D. PEOPLES: No. There was certainly a lot of back and forth and so on and so forth. It was not without disagreement or difficulty, but everything worked out. On these projects, I always find that, in the end, there's something that the writer wishes he had done a little differently and something the director wishes he had done a little differently and something the actors wish they had done a little differently. We all have a tendency to remember when we were right and carefully forget when we were wrong.

FROUG: True.

"I always find that, in the end, there's something that the writer wishes he had done a little differently and something the director wishes he had done a little differently and something the actors wish they had done a little differently."

D. PEOPLES: I try to discipline myself, but I must say there are some wonderful scenes in *Hero*, some wonderful moments in *Hero*, that I was adamantly outraged and opposed to. The actors pushed for them, Stephen agreed with them, and, boy, were the actors and Stephen right. And, boy, was I wrong.

FROUG: Amazing.

D. PEOPLES: Well, it's not amazing. I find it to be true very often.

FROUG: What I meant by amazing is that the writer admits that.

D. PEOPLES: But it's a fact. There's always a lot of back and forth. There were lines in *Hero* that people were always attacking, saying, "This could be better." And very often they're wrong and things get rewritten worse instead of better. But I remember a line in there that nobody was ever negative about, but I thought it was a terrible line. I thought, I've got to make this line better. And every time I tried, instead of getting better, it got worse.

FROUG: What was the line?

D. PEOPLES: It's a line where Bernie sits down and he says to Chick, the bartender, "You think you got problems, I've got all the problems." Something like that. It was an expository line. He had to introduce that for us, but it just embarrassed me. It was so flat and so stupid, but I never fixed it. I never knew how to fix it. Then I looked at the dailies, and when I heard it on the screen, I thought, That sounds like good writing. Dustin made it sound like good writing. The fact of the matter is, it's not good writing, it's Dustin Hoffman. He's just a great actor.

FROUG: There's no denying that. He is a great actor by any standard. But to a lot of people he is a pain in the ass to work with.

D. PEOPLES: There is this funny story about that, too. Stephen Frears said to me one day, "You know, Dustin Hoffman has a reputation for being difficult. But Dustin Hoffman isn't difficult, David, *you are*." What can I say?

FROUG: "What can you say?" is right.

D. PEOPLES: Everybody on that picture—Laura Ziskin, Stephen Frears, David Peoples, Dustin Hoffman, Geena Davis, Andy Garcia—was passionate about what we were doing. I'm really proud of that movie. I think it's terrific. That's the bottom line.

FROUG: How did you feel about *Blood of Heroes*?

D. PEOPLES: I thought the director should have been shot.

FROUG: You directed it, didn't you?

D. PEOPLES: Yeah, I directed that. I can't figure out which guy was to blame—the writer or the director. I was both. [Laughter] How am I going to say this with clarity? I'm actually very proud of the movie. I like the movie. I think the actors were all terrific. But I intended the movie to be absolutely overwhelmingly entertaining and I have to admit that after having seen it with audiences, it isn't absolutely overwhelmingly entertaining. I don't know whether to blame Dave Peoples the scriptwriter or Dave Peoples the director. I know that there is nobody else to blame because it was an absolutely sensational cast. They were fantastic in every sense. And I had a tremendous crew. But somehow, it's not as entertaining as it was supposed to be, and it doesn't quite move the way it was supposed to.

FROUG: Did it lead you to decide not to pursue a directing career and stick with writing?

D. PEOPLES: It was a very good experience. I learned so much from it. If I'd done it when I was twenty-seven years old and I could then just sit down and direct ten more pictures, I would have become a very, very good director. Since I directed it when I was forty-eight, it became clear to me that, at forty-eight, I couldn't start becoming a professional director in the sense that I'm a professional writer who has spent years and years practicing. But I can still bring something special as a director to something I have written or something I feel enormously close to.

FROUG: Are you working on such a project?

D. PEOPLES: Well, yeah. I'm suppose to direct the one that Jan and I have just written. I'm contractually committed there.

FROUG: Is it an original screenplay?

D. PEOPLES: It's adapted from a novel.

FROUG: Do you prefer adapting or do you prefer to start from scratch with originals?

D. PEOPLES: My favorite thing in the world is just sitting down and writing a spec script. But, as you know, the business is designed to tempt people to do something different than that, to either pitch or set up something that has already been published. That guarantees you a sale, but it limits your flexibility and your freedom. It's an economic thing. You make your choices, and I'm ashamed to say that I've not had the courage just to write nothing but spec scripts. I've been tempted and I've bitten the apple. Beyond that, I still prefer

"My favorite thing in the world is just sitting down and writing a spec script. But, as you know, the business is designed to tempt people to do something different than that, to either pitch or set up something that has already been published."

working from original stuff. But I guess it just depends. Janet and I are now starting an adaptation of James Dickey's latest novel because we got excited by it. It's called *To the White Sea*. It's so difficult as a movie. That's what attracted the both of us. It's totally impossible.

FROUG: You like the challenge?

D. PEOPLES: Yes, absolutely. It's terrifically challenging. It's a great book.

FROUG: Did you move up to Berkeley to get away from Hollywood?

D. PEOPLES: Quite the opposite. The joke is that, when Janet and I moved out here, we thought San Francisco and Los Angeles were twenty miles apart.

FROUG: Where did you come from?

D. PEOPLES: We came from the East Coast. We had friends up in the San Francisco area, so we settled up here and I went to school here and our children were born here. I worked as a film editor up here, and we just never got into sync about getting to Los Angeles. As time went on, my writing career went well enough that we no longer had any real pressure to move to Los Angeles. We love Los Angeles. We love the people down there. We love the movie industry and every-thing. But we've put certain roots here. We raised our children here. As it is now, we get to Los Angeles on business. Whereas, if we moved to Los Angeles, we'd never get up here.

FROUG: A lot of writers feel that if you move away from Hollywood, you don't have to put up with those endless meetings.

D. PEOPLES: The meetings are a huge negative.

FROUG: Why is it, once you finish a script, and you've done what you want and what they claim they want, they bring in someone else to rewrite it?

D. PEOPLES: Well, I don't know the answer to that. I don't think there is a simple answer to it. There is an insecurity aspect and there's also such a thing as writer burnout. Writers are asked to write and rewrite to the point of becoming less and less productive. But there is always the irony that, even though huge numbers of scripts are ruined rather than improved by the development process, sometimes scripts that go through these incredible version-after-version and writer-after-writer sagas come out quite good. That sort of ruins it for writers.

FROUG: It encourages more free-for-all rewriting.

D. PEOPLES: Some say a movie is going to be a disaster just because the script went through fifty writers. I think that you've got better odds if you can stay with fewer writers. But you can't guarantee it. It's not always wrong to replace a writer. It's just something that's done more frequently than necessary. People would do it with directors if it were economically feasible. They'd do it with actors if it were economically feasible. It just happens to be easier to replace writers than directors or actors. But they'll do it with anyone, if they can afford it.

FROUG: All this is a struggle for security, right?

D. PEOPLES: A struggle against insecurity. And I'm not singling out executives because it's difficult for producers, difficult for directors, difficult for actors, difficult for writers to stay focused on what is good about a project. When you go to see a movie, what gets you there is what's good about it and what keeps you there is what's good about it. Some of the movies we enjoy have the most incredible flaws in them. Now, I'm not saying it's good to have flaws, but if what you're trying to do is eliminate the flaws rather than simply minimize them and accentuate what's good, you get into a destructive spiral.

FROUG: Do you think that if writers get into a frenzy of rewriting, they never get finished?

D. PEOPLES: Yeah. They also tend to damage what's good while they continually chip away, trying to fix what's bad. There are times when what you have to do is focus on what's good, what works. I think that's the great thing that I so admire about what Clint Eastwood did in *Unforgiven*, because there are plenty of flaws to that screenplay and I don't think for a minute he was unaware of them. I could see things I didn't like about the way *Unforgiven* worked, but every time I tried to fix it, I made it worse. And when you get to that point, you have to back off and say, "Is this good or isn't it good?" And if it's good, you've got to button up and go with it. And if it isn't any good, you've got to put it aside. But you can't destroy it in order to try to make it better. To Clint's credit, he is a man of enormous artistic courage. Artistically, he's one of the ballsiest people out there. Look at his history of movies. I think he just says, "This is what I'm going to do; I know people might not like it and I know people might even laugh at it, but this is what I'm going to do." And he's made some good, good pictures. I think that *Bronco Billy* is a good example: a flawed movie, maybe, but an original with a great character in it.

FROUG: His stuff is often very daring and original.

D. PEOPLES: Yeah, it is. With *Unforgiven* he . . .

FROUG: He didn't touch a line, right?

D. PEOPLES: Well, I won't say that he didn't touch a line, but he understood every scene and he made every scene work the way it was intended to work. Little lines were changed here and there, but you can't not do that.

FROUG: He didn't bring in a rewrite person?

D. PEOPLES: No. As I say, I think that he said, "Okay, this is the script we're gonna make, warts and all." And where the page wasn't working, he made it work. I think that that's a great director and a really gutsy guy. You have to be able to shut out your doubts because you're always going to have doubts. I've got nothing but praise for him. He's got my undying respect.

FROUG: Let's bring in your partner. How long have you and Janet been partners?

D. PEOPLES: How long have we been married?

FROUG: Well, both. Yeah, while we're at it, how long have you been married?

J. PEOPLES: We've been married for thirty-six years and we started writing together on documentaries in the late-'70s.

FROUG: Jan, thank you for joining us. I don't want us to be accused of sexual discrimination.

J. PEOPLES: I wouldn't do that. I'm a great admirer of your work.

FROUG: Thank you, you're a sweetheart. What does the pressure of writing together do to your marriage? You and David must disagree on a lot of things.

D. PEOPLES: Oh, yes, absolutely.

FROUG: At what point did you two decide to collaborate as writers?

D. PEOPLES: Intermittently, we worked together on various projects starting in the '70s. We collaborate if it seems like a project we have a common interest in or that we would do better together. For example, Janet was an expert on J. Robert Oppenheimer and, when Jon Else came to us about doing a documentary on Oppenheimer, I was in on it too because I was a film editor.

FROUG: This was *The Day After Trinity*?

D. PEOPLES: Yes. That's always the way it's worked. And there are other things that are my ideas, and Jan's not the least bit interested in them and vice versa.

J. PEOPLES: We haven't actually collaborated on an original screenplay. We have our own original stories. We tend to collaborate on projects that people bring to us or books we're both interested in that might call for an adaptation to a screenplay. Very often, it's just that we have a mutual enthusiasm for some project. If we like the project and we like the people who have brought it to us, then we probably will be tempted to do it together if we're not too restricted by other projects. It's a lot of fun working together, collaborating, but you have a different kind of satisfaction when you're doing your own original work. Would you agree, Dave?

D. PEOPLES: Absolutely. What's interesting about the collaborative thing is that it's a whole different voice. We just wrote a screenplay together called *Twelve Monkeys*, which is in post-production now. It was inspired by the French film *La Jetée*; and I know there was no way I could have written a screenplay like that myself. It's not something I could have ever solved or done. I don't know how you feel, Jan, whether you could've written it yourself, but now it's a whole new thing. It's a David and Janet script as opposed to a Janet script or a David script. On that script, that was exactly the right thing to do and exactly the right way to do it. And I think it was a good script for that reason.

FROUG: Janet, what do you think it is that you bring to the script that David couldn't have done by himself?

J. PEOPLES: I'm not sure. I think that we're interested in different scenes and interested in slightly different approaches to certain scenes. I think that David is saying that he wouldn't have thought he could have done *Twelve Monkeys* on his own. But the reality is, once you start working on a project, you do find there's your own little voice in there in a collaborative way. It turned out to be very much a David script and a Janet script, which was very interesting to me. Friends of ours who have read it and the people who have worked with us before say that they can see both of us in this project. I think David thought it was more mine. It's a romance story. Although David does like love stories, he doesn't always say that he's writing them.

D. PEOPLES: I have no talent at all for writing a thriller, for example. That's something I couldn't do on my own.

J. PEOPLES: On the other hand, that is exactly where we are in the script we're working on right now, and you have very strong opinions on how to do this dramatically, David.

FROUG: Do you take scenes or do you take alternate sections? Does one of you say, "You do this and I'll do that"? How do you write?

J. PEOPLES: It's very organic. When we were doing *Twelve Monkeys*, we hammered out a story that delighted both of us. When we started writing, we each just started on the first act in our separate offices. Then we got together to see where we were. It was interesting to find what remained the same and what changed. Then one of us would say, "Oh, I like that in yours," "I like this," and vice versa. And the other one would say, "Oh, I don't like it as much as I like yours," or whatever. You start moving toward a consensus. But each project has been different. In some, we both start and just do the first act, because we don't know how to start. Or we each do it and then we see where we are. And then, maybe one of us will say, "Oh, why don't you go ahead with the second act and I'll start rewriting the first." Or maybe we'll say, "Let's work on this part." It's very organic. You agree, Dave?

D. PEOPLES: Yes. We find our way but, in the end, it's sort of a struggle. It's a struggle to write a script alone and it's a struggle to write a script collaboratively. There's no way around it.

FROUG: Do you plot your scripts carefully? Do you outline your screenplays?

"It's a struggle to write a script alone and it's a struggle to write a script collaboratively. There's no way around it."

D. PEOPLES: We outline pretty thoroughly but not exhaustively.

J. PEOPLES: I would say that we have to have the main scenes, although they may change. All the way along the line, we're careful to give ourselves and each other breathing room to come up with a newer way, a better way to do something.

FROUG: That sounds like the perfect collaboration.

J. PEOPLES: When it works!

FROUG: When it works? Nothing is perfect. Nothing works all the time. But you are equal partners, equally creative in the process?

D. PEOPLES: Yes. And we hammer back and forth so much that I don't know if I could find more than a sentence or two of *Twelve Monkeys*, for example, that I was sure came just from me. Wouldn't that be true of you too, Jan?

J. PEOPLES: Absolutely.

[*Twelve Monkeys* opened shortly after our interview. So I went back and asked Janet and David for their reaction to it. "Since our interview, *Twelve Monkeys* opened and is doing great, and we are delighted that so many people have gone to see it. We think that everyone connected with the film, especially Terry Gilliam, did an outstanding job, and we are more than a little proud of our own part in it." —D.W.P. and J.P.]

D. PEOPLES: We go back and forth, and in the end, we've worked it so much that we no longer have any sense of which one contributed what.

J. PEOPLES: If you write a screenplay by yourself, you think that everything's there, even though you know that you might not have accomplished everything that you set out to do. And when you finish it, you're amazed and horrified that in four or five places you have changed scenes and that there are holes—people couldn't understand main story points—and you have to reel back from this and start correcting it. You may, in fact, get a suggestion from somebody that takes you a whole different way. When you collaborate, you get that from your partner all the way through. You're not waiting for the very end. You're hammering and hammering and hammering and saying, "I don't understand" or "do you know why you did this?" or "what was the motivation?" or "what's your intention here?" You critique each other's work. At the same time, you try to preserve the best and move forward with the best. You find that you're really getting a lot accomplished by working collaboratively.

FROUG: Do you have to set your own egos aside in favor of this combined ego that makes this combined work?

D. PEOPLES: Well, yeah, that's the end result. But you don't just get to set them aside, you have to work out the drama. For example, shortly before you called, we were engaged in a rather heated discussion [Much laughter] about a scene in a script we're finishing up right now.

FROUG: This is part of your two-picture deal?

D. PEOPLES: Yes. It's called *The Grabbers*.

FROUG: Is this an original?

D. PEOPLES: No, *The Grabbers* is from a novel by Lester Taub.

FROUG: Do you find adapting novels to be pretty difficult?

D. PEOPLES: Well, we wouldn't do it unless there was something about the novel that excited us, that enticed us, that made us feel it was worth doing. We're fortunate enough that we have choices, so we haven't had to take jobs just because we had to eat. As a consequence, the ones we take are the ones that turn us on. As I mentioned, *To the White Sea* hooked us partly because it was so challenging and partly because it's a superb novel.

FROUG: What are the special problems of adapting a book?

J. PEOPLES: Well, I would suspect that if you were adapting a book that was very, very well known, you would have to make the decision whether to remain faithful to that author's audience. I don't want to sound pompous at all, but it's much easier to adapt a book if you don't have to remain loyal to other people's preconceptions of it. Don't you agree, David?

D. PEOPLES: Yeah, you have more latitude. Also, there is the fact, backed by history, that good books often don't make good movies and bad books often make better movies. I think it's probably because the forms are so different. If you are really using the novel and the things that the novel has to offer you, you're working against a movie. Whereas, if you're not using a novel in the fullest sense, sometimes it's easier to convert it to a movie. I don't know if that's true, but it's certainly something to speculate on.

FROUG: Let me paraphrase a very interesting statement from Bo Goldman. He said that when he started working with

"I don't want to sound pompous at all, but it's much easier to adapt a book if you don't have to remain loyal to other people's preconceptions of it."

[177]

Milos Forman on adapting *One Flew Over the Cuckoo's Nest*, Forman said to him, "Remember, this is a movie, not a book. Forget the book. What we've got to make is something different." And Bo said, "I approached it with Milos' insistence that we not recreate the book, and from then on, I was freed up to write whatever I wanted to write." You're doing this with the new book you're now adapting, *The Grabbers*, right?

D. PEOPLES: Yes. I think we've departed significantly from the book.

J. PEOPLES: The book is very story-driven. What we've done with it, if we've succeeded, is keep a lot of the main ingredients of the story but make it character-driven.

FROUG: Do you guys look forward to working on originals together or do you think this is the way the industry is going—adapting books because they are pre-sold, pre-tested material?

D. PEOPLES: We both want to continue to write originals because that's the most rewarding thing.

J. PEOPLES: I find that the most personally satisfying, which doesn't mean that any audience of mine would find that my originals are better. I do think that because David has achieved a little bit of recognition within the industry, more people bring projects and books and ideas to us. We feel that this is an opportunity, and we want to hear these people's ideas or see the books or the movies. I suspect that when you're starting, you do write originals because you're learning your craft and trying to gain an audience within the industry.

D. PEOPLES: I just think writing originals is the most rewarding thing. We hope that we won't always be tempted to do adaptations in any of our three voices—the David voice, the Janet voice, the David and Janet voice. All three ought to be writing originals and probably will, but we've been tempted by a few projects.

FROUG: Did anybody object when the David voice became the David and Janet voice? In other words, David, you have sole credit on *Unforgiven*, and you now have a status that is in the very upper echelon. When you said, "Janet and I are going to collaborate," did anybody say, "Wait a minute, we don't want a team, we want David Webb Peoples, the guy who wrote *Unforgiven*"?

J. PEOPLES: We were offered *Twelve Monkeys*, for instance, by a producer who had worked on projects with each of us. David had his deal at Universal and I had done a development project with Universal. I was not an unknown. The next time that people came to us, it was the exact same circumstance. It was somebody whom we both knew, somebody who knew both our work, and a studio that knew both our work. So we are established individually as screenwriters and as a team.

FROUG: I enjoy talking to you, Janet Peoples, David Peoples, and the team of Janet and David Peoples. You are three terrific screenwriters.

CREDITS

David Webb Peoples
The Day After Trinity (shared credit)
Blade Runner (shared credit)
Leviathan (shared credit)
Blood of Heroes (sole screenplay)
Unforgiven (sole story and screenplay) Academy Award
   nomination.
Hero (also called *Accidental Hero*) (sole screenplay)
Twelve Monkeys (shared screenplay)
The Grabbers (shared screenplay)

Janet Peoples
The Day After Trinity (shared screenplay)
Twelve Monkeys (shared screenplay)

The Iliad *is only great because all life is a battle,*
the Odyssey *because all life is a journey,*
the Book of Job because all life is a riddle.
—G.K. Chesterton, quoted by Burton Rascoe, *The Joys of Reading*

The inclination to digress is human. But the dramatist must avoid it
even more strenuously than the saint must avoid sin, for while the
sin may be venial, digression is mortal.
—W. Somerset Maugham, *The Summing Up*

Boredom, after all, is a form of criticism.
—William Phillips, *A Sense of the Present*

Promises, Promises!

Hollywood is an empire of ephemeral enthusiasms. It is as certain as air that what agents, studio execs, stars, producers, directors, et-al. fall madly in love with today often has little interest for them tomorrow. This is perhaps the most difficult lesson the screenwriter has to face throughout his or her career.

I had dinner recently with a top-level screenwriter buddy who is highly knowledgeable about the unpredictability and unreliability of the movers and shakers of the Hollywood filmmaking industry. He waxed enthusiastically about discussions he'd had with a big-as-they-come director who was interested in one of his screenplays: "He told me that he'd taken my screenplay with him on a recent overseas flight, and that after reading page one, he couldn't stop until he'd read it all. 'It's perfect,' he told me, 'it's going to be my next film. I'm not going to change a word of your screenplay, I'll just shoot it the way it is.'"

I gave my poor buddy a beating for swallowing that tired old Hollywood-style bullshit. But unconvinced by my jibes, he insisted that the director was on the level, that everything would happen just as the director assured him it would.

"Sure," I said, "and it's snowing right now in Sarasota."

A couple of weeks later, my friend phoned to tell me that the director had decided not to direct his screenplay, and that the director felt that he needed to change the protagonist's "arc."

(For those of you not up on the latest Hollywood catchphrase, "arc" means the development or evolution of a story or a character from the beginning of a screenplay through to the end. You're wise if you can throw in the word "arc" while discussing your story or screenplay with the pros. They love that stuff. While you're at it, I suggest you throw in some guru double-talk about "steps" or "story turns" or anything else that suggests you've read the current books on structure. It helps them feel a little more secure.)

If I had ten dollars for every time an important star, studio executive, director, or film nabob told me, "We love your screenplay, we're going into production as soon as we line up the star (or the director, or the location, or the studio backing, or a role of 35mm film)," I'd be a millionaire. Yet my good friend, now a seasoned, professional Hollywood screenwriter, and a man who is as intelligent as they come, fell for the Great Hollywood Cliché: "We Love Your Screenplay, We're Going To Shoot It Exactly As It Is."

Why would my pal fall for the oldest con in town? *Because it is not a con.* There's no doubt in my mind that the director was on the level, that he meant exactly what he was saying, what he was feeling, *at that moment in time.*

I tell you this cautionary tale to illustrate one of the most difficult and ongoing problems screenwriters in America must continually deal with. If you are at all competent, I can promise you that somebody will come along in the course of your career with the exciting announcement that your script is terrific and ready to shoot. You will possibly come away from this dose of hype feeling that, in the very near future, fame and fortune are coming your way. But most of the time, you are merely a victim of the *instant enthusiasm* of somebody eager to advance their own career, someone whose enthusiasm is genuine *at that moment in time*.

If you cannot accept this most basic quirk of moviemaking, you are in for a lot of disappointment and grief. And, worse yet, you can lead yourself down a dangerous path to depression.

I cannot overemphasize that these fits of enthusiasm and these promises are both genuine and empty, and that, in truth, most of them only result in an affirmation of your talent coupled with disappointment.

Quick sample story: I was assigned to write an episode of the then-popular TV series *Quincy*. After I turned in the script, the producer's secretary phoned to tell me that mine was the best script they had for the season. A week later the producer phoned and said, "I love it, we're shooting it next week."

Another week passed and the producer phoned me again: "Jack Klugman (the series' star) hated it, we're throwing the entire thing out. He says that there's no sense in doing a rewrite."

A month later, the producer called yet again: "Jack's decided that he would love to do the script if I'll do a rewrite."

Several week later, a copy of the script arrived at my home. It was rewritten to the point of non-recognition. Only the story was the same; most of the scenes were different. A note on it said that they were shooting it in a week. I phoned the producer and suggested that he take credit because there wasn't a word of mine left. He refused: "It's still basically your story; we just changed a couple of scenes. Jack is very excited about doing it. He says that it's going to be our best show."

When the episode appeared on the tube, I made a point of not watching it. (I still have not seen most of the shows I wrote for television.) Why aggravate an already aggravating experience?

Your only defense (and it's important that you develop it) is to take none of the hype seriously—it has the substance of cotton candy.

As the former Executive Producer in charge of Drama for CBS-TV, I've seen the following happen over and over again:

A writer comes into the office and pitches a story, and the response is, "Great, we love it, how soon can we have it?"

The writer leaves on a cloud of euphoria. But the executives who remain in the meeting room have the following discussion:

"That was a great idea, I think we ought to go with it."

"Agreed, but I'm not sure it has legs. I can see the first three or four episodes, maybe even six, but I don't think the idea will go the distance."

"Gee, come to think of it, you're right. Yep, it's a six-episode idea. Have business affairs call the writer's agent tomorrow and say that we love the idea but we've decided to pass."

Identical meetings take place all day, every day, in every Hollywood office. And whether the conversations are about movies or television series, the innocent victim is always the screenwriter.

To be fair, sometimes these meetings bear real fruit, but most of the time they are a waste of the writer's time. (Of course, the executives get *paid* to do this all day long.) This is one of the reasons that many established screenwriters do everything possible to avoid meetings. They know that most enthusiasms and opinions expressed during these meetings have the lifespan of a snowflake in hell. The pros learn that the enthusiasm is only real when your agent phones you and says, "The business affairs department phoned me. You have a deal; it's set." As the Writers Guild of America warns you, nothing is real in Hollywood *until your agent officially tells you he or she has closed a deal. You must not write or rewrite a line until you receive that notification.*

Promises in Hollywood are as empty as the air you breathe . . . and just as pure. Be forewarned: This is a serious problem, especially for writers, the most frequent victims. If rejection doesn't kill you, momentary enthusiasms very well might *unless you refuse to take them seriously.*

P.S. When I last spoke with my screenwriter buddy, whose Hollywood courting dance I described at the top of this piece, he was giving a full-court press to rewriting his screenplay because the director has now decided that he might direct it after all if my pal does a rewrite that both the director and the major star (who may or may not decide to be in the film) like.

These unofficial negotiations have been known to drag on for months or even years, and it's always the screenwriter who ends up busting his butt to please a possible buyer. (Although the Writers Guild specifically forbids rewriting on spec, recognize that screenwriters, like everybody else, gets caught up in their own enthusiasms.) And after all the hype and bullshit, the screenwriter's one truth is that the mortgage has to be paid.

Another Road,
a Different Journey

Hollywood is by no means the only route for an aspiring screen-writer to take. It's been over thirty years since a self-described house-wife and her husband in the suburbs of Cleveland, Frank and Eleanor Perry, set out to make their own film. Eleanor, an avid filmgoer, had read a brief, published, case history of a couple of teenagers hospi-talized with mental disorders. She knew there was a movie in it and that she had to write the screenplay. The Perrys raised the money for their film by convincing their well-to-do doctor friends and neigh-bors that moviemaking is a good investment.

Though inexperienced, it turned out that Eleanor was a first-class screenwriter and her husband was a first-class director. The little independent movie they made back in 1962 was called *David and Lisa*, and it became an instant classic. It cost about $180,000, grossed over one million in its first U.S. run, and has been running periodically ever since. With the added income from cable, cassettes sales, video rentals, et al., the investors did quite handsomely.

Frank and Eleanor both won Academy Award nominations and each went on to big careers in Hollywood, jointly and separately, with many major films to their credit. Eleanor and I were good friends when we were both working on the lot at MGM. During one of our many lunches together in the commissary, she asked me, rhetorically, "How does a bored housewife, living in a suburb of Cleveland, end up in Hollywood writing *The Man Who Loved Cat Dancing*?" Answering her own question, she said, "You write a screenplay, then you get out and hustle the money to make the picture yourself, that's how." And she added with a rueful smile, ". . . and now I'm having the worst writing experience of my life." (Some of Eleanor's experiences as a Hollywood screenwriter were less than pleasant. She wrote a bitter account of writing *The Man Who Loved Cat Dancing* in her book *Blue Pages*. It's a very good, but not uncommon, example of a Hollywood screenwriter's nightmare.)

The Perrys, as it turned out, were thirty years ahead of their time. Frank and Eleanor were among the first of a whole new school of young filmmakers who have discovered that the quickest and best way to begin a big-time career as a screenwriter is to *raise the money and make the movie yourself.*

Is raising money to make a movie easy? Do birds bark? For some people it is quite impossible. But for many others—those with the talent to sell themselves and their vision—it's easier than the struggle to establish themselves in the cold, unwelcome world of Hollywood that every newcomer faces.

Certainly the most startling independent film of recent years is *El Mariachi*, which Robert Rodriguez made for a budget of $7,000! Rodriguez wrote, directed, photographed, edited, and co-produced this film. Now we are really talking the rare instance of an authentic auteur. Even amateur actors were used for this remarkable film, which not only won awards but launched Rodriguez on a big-time career.

Other recently successful, independently produced, low-budget films include *El Norte*; *Gas, Food, Lodging*; *Smoke*; and *Clerks*. I could fill a book with the number of young filmmakers (including screenwriters) who have achieved industry and audience recognition by going the low-budget, independent route. It's something every new screenwriter ought to evaluate as one of his or her options.

Thanks to Robert Redford, who made his film debut as the fastest gun in the West in *Butch Cassidy and The Sundance Kid*, there is now the remarkable Sundance Institute of the Arts, where young and not-so-young filmmakers have a chance to get help in developing their screenplays, and the opportunity to show their films before an audience of Hollywood's elite.

The screening of independent films sponsored by Sundance Institute is now a yearly sellout, with Hollywood movers and shakers fighting to get tickets. Many young filmmakers are now in the process of building important careers thanks to the visionary concept of an actor-director—Redford—who wholeheartedly believes that he should give back to the film world what the film world gave him.

Consider these career-launching Sundance winners: *sex, lies and videotapes*; *Before Sunrise*; *Citizen X*; *Red Rock West*; *Passion Fish*; *Buffalo Girls*; *Boca*; *Ruby in Paradise*; *Reservoir Dogs*; *Caged Hearts*; and *Colonel Chabert*. These movies opened doors for screenwriters, directors, and producers.

But lest you draw a rosy picture of certain glory and success, for every low-budget, independent film Sundance accepts for screening, scores are turned away. Redford has said that the biggest problem with these rejected films is poor screenplays. So Sundance is now offering screenwriting workshops twice a year. Here, aspiring screenwriters have an opportunity to work one-on-one with top-ranked professional screenwriters such as Steven Zaillian (*Schindler's List, Searching for Bobby Fischer*) and the many other pros who fly into Sundance at their own expense to help the newcomers.

Today the competition to get a screening at the Sundance Film Festival is very tough, and it's not easy to make it into their excellent screenwriters' workshops.

But let me cite an example of the good news: Edward Burns wrote, directed, executive produced, and starred in a low-budget film called *The Brothers McMullen*. It won the top prize at the Sundance Film Festival, and deservedly so. It's an unpretentious, delightful, and charming film. It was shot in Burns' parent's home on a minuscule budget, with a film crew you could count on your fingers. Burns created not only the film but a new and promising career.

If you have a completed screenplay that you truly believe in, I suggest you request a submission form for one of the Sundance Institute's screenwriting workshops. It could change your life and set you off on a new and exciting road. Frank and Eleanor Perry didn't have the Sundance Institute back in 1962, but seven years later, The Sundance Kid came to Utah with a brand new concept and a creative vision that changed the face of filmmaking for the foreseeable future.

About Screenwriting "Rules"

In writing and directing *The Brothers McMullen*, young Edward Burns broke every screenwriting teacher's "rules": *The movie has almost no conflict*. The structure is loose, easy, relaxed, formless. There are no "big" scenes. There is no violence, obscenity, or big plot twists. Burns announces his theme in the first scene: Follow your heart and make a commitment to love, if and when you find it, in spite of all obstacles.

Burns proved, yet again, that movies are about telling interesting stories. That's the key to any successful narrative film. What Burns had, which I consider among the most important elements in a great screenplay, was a strong, universal theme—a theme with which everybody in the world can identify.

In the opening scene, at the funeral of their father, the mother of three Irish-American brothers announces that, after thirty-five years of living with their abusive, alcoholic father, she's returning to Ireland to marry the man she has truly loved all of her life.

The three sons are immediately plunged into the issue of love and the commitment that it requires. The film is woven around this single theme, which *unifies the film and is also the action line.* (As screenwriters, you are always ahead of the game when you have a universal theme. And what could be more universal than the obstacles we struggle with before making a commitment to true love?) The film explores how this issue affects these funny, delightfully confused young men who are at crossroads in their lives. *The movie is almost entirely conversation*—the brothers "talk story" with wit and charm. But it's attention-getting conversation because we all understand the difficulty of defining and making a commitment to "true love."

Another important reason why this film, rich with humor, won acclaim at Sundance, and later in general release, is that each of these brothers is a three-dimensional character—alive, perhaps a little eccentric, but believable and fascinating.

Edward Burns proves that you don't need violence or obscenity to engage an audience. He could well become a harbinger of movies about average guys and women who are struggling with universal problems that have been with us since the dawn of recorded history.

Rent the videotape and see something different and refreshing. Prove to yourself that there are no rules about how to write a screenplay. (Of course, some self-appointed guru, no doubt a member of the Moon Is Blue Cheese Society, will come along and explain to you that there are 27, 32, 21, 39, whatever "steps" that make the movie work.)

The blunt truth is that no professional screenwriter writes with "steps" in his or her head. And neither should beginners. *You* are the "rules." You create your own screenplay, not by following somebody's formula, but by following your own gut instincts. Don't let anybody or anything block what's going on inside you, eager to be expressed. It's your own personal, private Muse. The single most important gift you must bring to your screenplay is writing what you feel deeply about. Very likely what you are about is what every human on this planet is about.

Walter Brown Newman, in *The Screenwriter Looks at the Screenwriter*, said: "I am really not interested in the problems that you read about in the newspapers. I'm interested in the problems that have nothing to do with those things. I'm interested in how you meet life, how you meet death, how you meet love, how you meet hate, how you express these things, what you do about them, what you do about dignity, your own, what you do about integrity, how you hang on to it, when you let go, what does it mean to compromise, is it wise, ever? I have a feeling these things engaged the people while they were building the pyramids. And, without being stuffy about it and not by any means thinking of myself in terms of the great Greeks or anything like that, I find naturally that these are the things that interest me."

All the drama you need is in your own life, in your own experiences. You are a bottomless well of experiences and emotions, and as a screenwriter, the place to put them is in your script. The job you have is to dig down inside yourself and discover as much about who you are and what you feel as is possible, then bring it up to the surface, examine it, and see how to put it to work for you. That, my friends, is how you will find your screenplay . . . and many, many more to follow.

You have to approach screenwriting with confidence. And nobody does that better than the aspiring filmmaker who goes out, raises the money, makes his or her own film, and becomes the artist he or she aspires to be. Sure, there's always the risk of failure, but all creativity rests on a willingness to take risks. Screenwriting is not only about creativity, it is also about bravery.

The Butcher Who Minted Millions

"**I**n those days we were called 'butchers,'" J. C. Hall explained to me as he took me on a guided tour of his Kansas City factory.

"There were 'news butchers' and 'candy butchers.' I was a 'postcard butcher,'" he continued. "We were traveling salesman who rode the trains from St. Louis to Kansas City and back, walking up and down the aisles, selling our wares. My business was very good; I sold postcards for a penny each. At the turn of the century, that was good money; a man could support his family. My business boomed until one day my supplier handed me a box of several hundred postcards of a new kind. They were made in France. They had pictures of women in corsets, bustles, petticoats—you could see *their ankles and their legs!* Pretty racy for the early 1900s."

As Hall and I strolled about his Hallmark Greeting Card plant, I saw giant machines spinning out greeting cards by the countless thousands, coming off the presses like sheets of money rolling out of the mint. It *is* a mint, I told myself, these Hallmark cards are money in the bank.

"The so-called dirty French postcards killed my business," Hall continued. "Husbands took them home and their wives raised the devil, refusing to allow them in the house. Then the men got mad at me for selling them, which finally put me out of the 'postcard butcher' business altogether. It turned out to be a blessing. Thanks to that experience, I went into the greeting-card business. Hallmark now sells more greeting cards than all the other greeting-card companies in the world combined."

"So you're minting money," I responded, indicating the presses.

"Yes, thanks to the 'dirty' French postcards, we're minting money, and I learned a lesson that has guided me all of my life."

In the mid-'50s, I was producing and directing "CBS Radio's Hallmark Hall of Fame," sponsored by J.C. Hall and his company.

When I took over, I drastically changed the format of the long-running series from historical drama to contemporary stories, luring the very shy, then-Major Chuck Yaeger to narrate the story of his breaking the sound barrier, convincing Ira Gershwin to narrate the story of his brother's untimely death, getting Joe DiMaggio to narrate the story of former Yankee manager Miller Huggins, having General Dean tell us of his capture and imprisonment during the Korean War. Every week we did segments from the lives of contemporary heroes narrated by either themselves or someone who knew them. The ratings soared and we quickly became the top-rated drama in those days of waning live-radio drama. For the moment, I was my sponsor's fair-haired boy. Hence my invitation to come to Kansas City to meet J. C. Hall and be shown the fountain from which the millions flowed.

"My ad agency," J.C. Hall confided, "wants me to stop sponsoring Shakespeare on TV and buy a cops-and-robbers show instead. I refused and they're furious with me. They have market surveys proving my approach is all wrong. They may be right, but I'm going my own way, and nobody can talk me out of it.

"My life as a postcard butcher taught me that the road to success is won by appealing to the highest level of our culture, not by pandering to the lowest common denominator. Sure, Shakespeare earned us only a five rating, or maybe even less. I don't care. That meant maybe five million people were watching my show, and they were really interested in Shakespeare. I'd rather have five million people who are seriously interested in my program than twenty-five million who watch it just to kill time. Besides, I really like Shakespeare.

"That's why we came up with our slogan," Hall continued, 'When You Care Enough To Send The Very Best.' Hallmark is going to stand for class, first and foremost, as long as I'm alive. I will not put my name on trash."

J. C. Hall steadfastly refused to follow the mob. He bought Sunday night prime-time on network TV for quality drama. The ratings were poor, but he didn't care. No amount of urging by his ad agency or the networks could convince him to sponsor anything less than the highest quality programming he could buy. He refused to follow the herd. He built an empire by ignoring the advice of all the experts. No wonder I took an immediate liking to him.

"Did you know," he asked rhetorically, "that more people go to see Shakespeare's plays than attend baseball games? And more people attend concerts and symphonies than sports events?"

The network saw to it that Hall's heretical views were stamped out abruptly. When he refused to change to popular, formulaic programming, they kicked him off the air! The networks claimed his high-mindedness was hurting their entire week's ratings. They not only took away his time period, they refused to allow him to sponsor any other regular prime-time period.

Today, decades later, Hall's heirs are having the last laugh—their greeting-card business is the mightiest enterprise of its kind in the world. And they still sponsor quality television programming with Hallmark specials three or four evenings a year. (Now the network welcomes their business . . . in prime time!) And Hallmark still holds to their founder's principal of putting on the highest quality programs, ratings be damned.

H.L. Menken reportedly said, "Nobody ever went broke underestimating the taste of the American public." Certainly Hollywood and the networks have thrived following that credo. But J.C. Hall followed the opposite path and made his own mint. When he and I completed our tour of his factory and returned to his office, he said, "My friends who are CEOs of the really big American companies tell me privately that they hate the junk their companies sponsor. In fact, they won't let their kids watch most of it. Me, I get up every morning, look in the mirror as I shave, and I'm proud of what I'm doing. Do you know how good that feels?"

Of course, that was a long time ago, before the current flood of vomit and excrement movies and a long time before television took over the world's screens. It was an era when people felt a genuine desire to be *proud of their work.*

Today, all that has changed. We now have filmmakers who are proud of how much *money* they're paid to put crap on the world's screens. (Privately, most of them cynically admit it's crap.) The newspeak of the '90s is expletives, occasionally sprinkled with lame jokes, as heroes splatter their victims' brains on shattered windshields while cars crash at high speed to the sound of ear-splitting "music." Audiences watch with glee as heroes, while cracking jokes, riddle their fellow humans with bullets. Seeing this mayhem and grand-scale slaughter, audiences are led to believe that countless maimed bodies bathed in buckets of blood is funny.

We have become dehumanized and anesthetized to vulgarity, violence, and obscenity. "You don't understand," a major director who is also my close friend carefully explained to me, *"it's all comedy."* I guess I need a laugh track to remind me. All too often, today's movies and television are a disgrace to the human spirit.

But what the hell, if you can make a few million bucks degrading human dignity, why not? It's a free country, and the First Amendment protects you from everybody but yourself.

Yet ask yourselves, Why write garbage you won't allow your own children to see? Or write screenplays that you laughingly apologize to your friends for writing, while bragging about the millions they paid you? It's Hollywood's biggest in-joke. Your bank account and your self-ridicule won't let you off the hook. I know many screenwriters and directors who, while they boast about their paychecks, they feel shame inside. Like J.C. Hall, they, too, have to look in the mirror when they shave. What are they seeing?

"Eternal vigilance is not only the price of liberty; eternal vigilance is the price of common decency."
—Aldous Huxley (from his introduction to the CBS Radio broadcast of my production and adaptation of his *Brave New World*, 1965)

Words strain,
Crack and sometimes break, under the burden,
Under the tension, slip, slide, perish,
Decay with imprecision, will not stay in place,
Will not stay still.
—T.S. Eliot, *Four Quartets*

The writer's intention hasn't anything to do with what he
achieves. The intent to earn money or the intent to become
famous or the intent to be great doesn't matter in the end.
Just what comes out.
—Lillian Hellman, from *Writers at Work, 3rd Series*

The maker of a sentence launches out into the infinite and
builds a road into Chaos and old Night.
—Ralph Waldo Emerson, *Journals*

A Gentle, Shy, Modest Lady with a Powerful Pen

An Interview with

Ruth Prawer Jhabvala

"They kept saying no, no; and they explained to us that if it were a seven-million-dollar film, okay. But this was a twenty-million-dollar film, and in a twenty-million-dollar film, the boy has to get the girl. So we parted."

—Ruth Prawer Jhabvala

In this book of interviews with highly individual and uniquely talented screenwriters, Ruth Prawer Jhabvala stands out as a singular and distinguished voice. Ms. Jhabvala has not only written eighteen films, she's published twelve novels and five collections of short stories, winning many literary prizes along the way, as well as two Oscars for best screenplay adapted from other material and a nomination for a third. She has also won a Writers Guild Award (Best Screenplay, *A Room with a View*), and two Guild nominations (*Howard's End* and *Remains of the Day*). This year she was awarded the Writers Guild of America's Foundation Career Achievement Award.

Along with her creative partners, producer Ismail Merchant and director James Ivory, she has turned out a body of work that has earned a permanent niche in the history of motion pictures. Such films as *A Room with a View*, *Mr. & Mrs. Bridge*, *Howard's End*, and *Remains of the Day* have made this team synonymous with the word "classic." Though some critics have called their leisurely paced style of movies boring, there is an ardent and sizable audience eagerly awaiting the release of each of their new works. And rightly so.

Ms. Jhabvala's screenplays remind us of a more civilized era when audiences did not need to be blasted with ruthless, ear-splitting, stereo-enhanced violence and vulgarized and trivialized sex, all awash with obscene language, apparently in the filmmakers' belief that they cannot hold an audience's attention otherwise. Merchant-Ivory-Jhabvala go their own way, creating high-quality costume dramas that have been bucking current movie trends for the past thirty-plus years. As a consequence, audiences and awards continue to follow them.

Ms. Jhabvala is a strong-minded but shy woman who zealously protects her privacy and, at age sixty-eight, continues to write either screenplays or novels seven days a week. She lives in New York City with her husband of forty-four years, Indian architect C.S.H. Jhabvala. As you will observe, she is an exceedingly modest and self-effacing woman. She lets her extraordinary work speak for itself.

FROUG: Ruth, I read that you had three children and three published novels by the age of thirty. How in the world did you handle it?

JHABVALA: Well, I was in India and I had a lot of help—domestic help, servants.

FROUG: Where were you raised?

JHABVALA: I was born in Germany, but I left for England when I was twelve. I grew up and went to school in England.

FROUG: So all your novels are written in English?

JHABVALA: Yes.

FROUG: Were you in England during the Blitz?

JHABVALA: Yes. I was a child in school, and yet I certainly remember it. I remember reading *Gone With the Wind* in a bomb shelter.

FROUG: What led you to leave the reasonably safe world of novels and venture into the risky and sometimes treacherous world of screenplays?

JHABVALA: I have never left the world of novels; I write novels continuously. I have as many novels as I have screenplays. I got into screenplays by accident—Merchant-Ivory bought one of my novels and asked me to adapt it.

FROUG: That was *The Householder*?

JHABVALA: *The Householder*, published in 1960. That was my first screenplay.

FROUG: Your films have a European flavor and yet I wonder if you were influenced by Satyajit Ray's films in India?

JHABVALA: I'm not, but I think James Ivory was influenced by Ray.

FROUG: Back in the '60s, he was one of my favorite filmmakers. I get a feeling of Ray from many of your movies where you gradually explore the interior of your characters. Do you indicate the close-ups in your screenplays that get us intensely involved in what's going on in the character's head?

JHABVALA: No, I indicate very little in my screenplays. I just put down the dialogue and minimal direction. I put down what the characters are thinking, that's all.

FROUG: In *Remains of the Day*, there's that marvelous scene where Emma Thompson, the housekeeper, approaches the head butler, Anthony Hopkins, who is reading a book, and she ways, "Let me see your book." He's terrified. He responds like she's prying into his private life. Did you indicate in your script that that's the way you wanted it played?

JHABVALA: No. I don't consciously put down anything. I put down the dialogue and what the characters are feeling at a certain moment if the dialogue requires it. I don't go into any detail.

FROUG: You've been working with Merchant-Ivory since the beginning. Have you become a partner with them?

JHABVALA: Do you mean a business partner?

"I put down the dialogue and what the characters are feeling at a certain moment if the dialogue requires it ."

FROUG: Yes.

JHABVALA: No.

FROUG: So you are still, in effect, employed to write a screenplay?

JHABVALA: Well, I'm not really quite sure I would say employed. For years, I just wrote screenplays on spec, hoping that they would get the money to do them. And usually they did.

FROUG: All three of you started together?

JHABVALA: Yes. We didn't have any money, so I didn't expect payment for a screenplay before they got the money for the picture together. I just wrote on spec.

FROUG: And this was while you were in India?

JHABVALA: Yes, and in New York, also.

FROUG: Do you live part-time in India and part-time in New York?

JHABVALA: Mostly New York. I go to India once a year.

FROUG: When you began screenwriting, did you study any screenplays?

JHABVALA: Not at all. I'd never read one in my life, and I hadn't seen that many films, either.

FROUG: So it's just intuition on your part?

JHABVALA: Well, you know, I don't find it that difficult. I don't think there's anything mysterious about writing a screenplay. If you're a writer, you know the story or the novel you're working from and how to put scenes together, how to write a scene for a character, a scene for structure. I think that's what's important.

FROUG: Mostly, you have adapted novels, including your own. Do you find novels a great source for screenplays?

JHABVALA: Well, it just happened that way. I've written quite a few original screenplays, too, but I just love some novelists like Henry James and Forster. They speak to the personality of the director I work with, James Ivory, extremely well. I write the screenplay and show it to him and he tells me mostly what he doesn't like . . . and then I redo it. And it might take over a period of two years or so. In earlier days we were more in a hurry. Now it does carry on for quite a long time.

FROUG: In my mind, you have established your own genre of films. You have defied the conventional wisdom that says that to get dramatic tension you must have sex and/or violence. And yet your most successful films—*Howard's End, Remains of the Day, Mr. & Mrs. Bridge, A Room with a View*—have become classics and have no overt sex nor violence.

JHABVALA: Well, they are all wonderful, wonderful books. We all love books. We draw much from rich material. Also none of these particular books is contemporary.

FROUG: You are saying that we will relate to anything that is human, no matter what period of history we're dealing with? The human species hasn't changed that much in the last thousand years or so?

JHABVALA: [Laughs] Yes, and that's what one relies on. It is especially difficult to run with the current tide of fashion. So we just go our own way.

FROUG: Do you work every day?

JHABVALA: Yes.

FROUG: Seven days a week?

JHABVALA: Yes. Usually. Except when I travel.

FROUG: When did you first start writing?

JHABVALA: When I was a child. When I was twenty-five, my first novel, *Amrita*, was published. It was published in New York City in '56. And England in '55.

FROUG: Have your films influenced the sales of your novels?

JHABVALA: No, not really. They never sold very well.

FROUG: But you're a writer because you are a writer. It's not a matter of choice, really, is it?

JHABVALA: No, it's not. I don't and I can't do anything else.

FROUG: Have you always known, even as a child, that you were a writer?

JHABVALA: Well, yes, I have. I was never good at anything else.

FROUG: It's good enough to have written eighteen films and I don't know how many novels.

JHABVALA: Seventeen books—twelve novels and five collections of short stories.

FROUG: That's a pretty prolific output.

JHABVALA: Yes. But it's been going on for forty years. It's a lifetime. I think, if you look at most writers, they do have quite a prolific output. If you write your whole life long, it adds up.

FROUG: Do you outline everything you write?

JHABVALA: Yes. I outline but I never stick to the outline.

FROUG: Do you write with a computer?

JHABVALA: I write in longhand and then I type it out. I type really badly but I type it out. I used to have a manual typewriter, but those aren't made any more so I got a computer, which I

"I outline but I never stick to the outline."

use as an ordinary typewriter or word processor and nothing more. I like it, actually.

FROUG: Were you happy with *Jefferson in Paris*?

JHABVALA: I was extremely happy with *Jefferson in Paris* and extremely unhappy with the reception it got. And I don't understand it to this day.

FROUG: Did you like Nick Nolte as Jefferson?

JHABVALA: I loved Nick Nolte. I thought he brought just the right element to Jefferson. You know, everyone tells us he was a refined aristocrat but he wasn't, he was a gentleman farmer. Nick Nolte brought just the right amount of roughness, you know, civilized but a man of the soil in many ways. Nolte had just that quality and was so American.

FROUG: Does critical disapproval very much affect a film today?

JHABVALA: Very much. If it's widespread, it's calamitous. And it could sink a film.

FROUG: Do you think it sunk *Jefferson in Paris*?

JHABVALA: It did sink it . . . yes, I think so. It still played a few months here because Disney stuck with it so marvelously: they advertised it, did everything they possibly could.

FROUG: What are you working on now?

JHABVALA: I've been doing a film about Picasso. But I really don't like to talk about current work.

FROUG: I tell my students that they shouldn't talk about what they are working on.

JHABVALA: I've heard it's bad luck.

FROUG: It dissipates the energy to do the work, I think.

JHABVALA: What I would like to do is one of the great Henry James novels, the ones from the end of his life—*The Ambassador, Wings of the Dove, The Golden Bowl.*

FROUG: Are you going to have any problems with your material now that Disney seems to own the entertainment world?

JHABVALA: No, I don't think so. We've only done one film for them so far, and they never once made any suggestions to change anything. They did their best to release it in the best possible way. They've been wonderful.

FROUG: Well, you're a very lucky screenwriter. Very few screenwriters can say that.

JHABVALA: I know. We have been extremely lucky. I hear about the other people's bad luck, but it certainly hasn't struck us ever. Warners is being very supportive of us with Picasso. We've just had good luck.

FROUG: It may not be that. It may be they recognize there's an audience for quality motion pictures and they give them the respect that is their due.

JHABVALA: I think, especially because the budgets are extremely reasonable, nobody is risking that much. The only time I came across problems with a studio's attempts to change a screenplay was when I'd written a screenplay in which, unlike the book, the boy didn't get the girl at the end. These studio people kept insisting that the boy must get the girl. They couldn't get it out of their heads. They kept saying no, no; and they explained to us that if it were a seven-million-dollar film, okay. But this was a twenty-million-dollar film, and in a twenty-million-dollar film, the boy has to get the girl. So we parted.

"The only time I came across problems with a studio's attempts to change a screenplay was when I'd written a screenplay in which, unlike the book, the boy didn't get the girl at the end."

[217]

FROUG: Rather than change it, you said no thank you? That kind of integrity is a very rare thing, believe me.

JHABVALA: To tell you the truth, we got paid. They couldn't get out of their contract with us.

FROUG: But I mean holding to your principles.

JHABVALA: It would have been ludicrous otherwise. Absolutely ludicrous.

FROUG: If you're not a partner business-wise, creatively you are a partner of the company, aren't you?

JHABVALA: Oh, yes. Usually I'm writing ahead. I usually have the screenplay quite a long time before they are ready to start shooting. They have other films to do. I never really choose the screenplay they want to do. I might push a novel in Jim's direction, but I'm not the one who actually chooses the subject. If I want to choose the subject, I do it for myself, I write a novel. But films should be what the director wants to do.

FROUG: Ivory picks which novels you're going to do next?

JHABVALA: I might make suggestions . . . I read a lot more than they do, or used to in the past. I've really introduced him to the novels of Henry James that might be good for us. And the same with Forster—we started with *A Room with a View*, but I always wanted to do *Howard's End*, but we couldn't get the money for it.

FROUG: *A Room with a View* was a magnificent movie. That was '84. Daniel Day Lewis gave a startling performance. When you saw it, were you surprised by what he brought to it?

JHABVALA: Yes, I was.

FROUG: You really live a private life. You pretty much stay out of the Hollywood scene, don't you?

JHABVALA: I stay out of the Hollywood scene physically, but we have our agent there. We're not entirely cut off from it, but we live our lives apart.

FROUG: Many highly successful screenwriters I've recently talked with prefer to live away from the studio scene. You don't get that kind of interference, do you? Where they constantly demand meetings about the screenplay?

JHABVALA: No, no, no. Nobody ever asks for a meeting about the screenplay.

FROUG: So once your trio agrees on a project and has the screenplay to go with, the studios either agree to finance it or they don't. In other words, there's no tinkering around with the script or bringing in rewriters.

JHABVALA: If they do, we go away. For years we couldn't get money for *Howard's End*. We got the most preposterous suggestions from people who were willing to put up money. So we would walk away, hoping we could find money elsewhere.

FROUG: It's a rare story, Ruth, believe me.

JHABVALA: It's mainly due to the producer Ismail Merchant, who is smart enough, and could always squeeze money out of a stone; he squeezed money out of a stone for years and years before we could establish relationships with people who understood what we wanted to do.

FROUG: It really is a big tribute to all three of you that you exercise that kind of an integrity and determination. You're like a little independent studio making your own kind of films.

JHABVALA: Yes. Such a happy relationship. But we do our films on a fairly modest budget.

FROUG: What do you call a modest budget?

JHABVALA: Well, *Jefferson* was the most expensive at fourteen million, which isn't much for a film like that.

FROUG: Among the films you've done, which is your favorite?

JHABVALA: *Mr. & Mrs. Bridge*, with Joanne Woodward and Paul Newman, is my favorite. It's a marvelous book.

FROUG: One thing your films all seem to have in common is a great theme. The theme of longing for relationships but being unable to have relationships in *Remains of the Day*. The driving for social status in *Howard's End*.

JHABVALA: We like to have very good material to start with. I've been able to take some very good novels and turn them into films.

FROUG: Taking it from the beginning, who do you think is the person most responsible for translating a novel into film?

JHABVALA: I can't really say. If the screenplay is really not good, if there's nothing sufficient to work with, then nothing can be done. But to me, finally, a film is the director's. The screenplay is only a blueprint for the film, something upon which other people have to build.

FROUG: But doesn't the selection of the scenes from the book and the characters on which to place emphasis come from the screenwriter?

JHABVALA: Yes. But if the directors or the actors or anybody along the line makes a mess of it, you could write the most wonderful scene in the world and nothing will happen.

FROUG: Have you had any that you felt they'd made a mess of?

JHABVALA: Every film has scenes that seemed terribly good on paper, but just came out so terribly. You can't always be certain what will work. It happens in every film, so I can well imagine that if you have a bad director or anyone along the line who does a poor job, it's really going to ruin you.

FROUG: A director can't make a great film from a poor screenplay?

JHABVALA: No. But the other way around, also.

FROUG: A director can make a dreadful film out of a very good screenplay?

JHABVALA: Yes, he can.

FROUG: Because the three of you, Merchant-Ivory-Jhabvala, have such a good relationship, you must have a shorthand that's really working for you by now.

JHABVALA: More or less. I know the sort of scenes that Jim really does well, and those I really like to write.

FROUG: You're obviously very good at it. I think there are probably few screenwriters working today who have your kind of record. You've kept your integrity and your art. When you see what the other screenwriters in this book have gone through, you will say, "My God, am I lucky."

JHABVALA: I know. I've heard so many rumors of what other people have to go through.

FROUG: I think your good fortune comes from your integrity.

JHABVALA: It also comes from having my two partners, who go through much more than I do. I mean they go out and fight. I don't do that; I don't have to go out.

FROUG: I believe that every screenwriter would love to be able to bring his or her art to a project unhampered by interference, as you do.

JHABVALA: We've been very lucky, I'm sure.

FROUG: You bring a lot of sensitivity to your works, which I find lacking in an awful lot of screenwriting. How do you do it?

"You can really only learn writing by writing."

JHABVALA: When people ask me how to become a screenwriter, I tell them to learn to tell stories. Learn to create characters. Know how they will react under certain conditions and certain circumstances and know how they interact with each other. Learn to write credible dialogue. All that sort of thing. You can really only learn writing by writing. Write and write and write. At least that's been my way. I know other screenwriters have come to it differently, probably with much more interest in films than I ever had. I never even thought of making films.

FROUG: As a child growing up in England, you weren't able to see a lot of movies?

JHABVALA: Well, you know, I spent my childhood in Germany until I was twelve, and Jews weren't allowed to go to the movie houses. After I moved to England, I saw films during the war. We would stand for hours in lines. But I wasn't that big a moviegoer. Then I went to India and I didn't see any films for almost ten years.

FROUG: Nonetheless, you successfully wrote screenplay after screenplay.

JHABVALA: From learning to write novel after novel. That's the way I came to it.

FROUG: I can't imagine a more successful way. I stand in awe.

JHABVALA: Thank you.

CREDITS

Novels:
To Whom She Will, 1955 (*Amrita* in the U.S.)
Nature of Passion, 1956
Esmond in India, 1958
The Householder, 1960
Get Ready for Battle, 1963
A Backward Place, 1965
A New Dominion (*Travelers* in the U.S.)
Heat And Dust, 1975
In Search of Love and Beauty, 1983
Three Continents, 1987
Poet and Dancer, 1993
Shards of Memory, 1995

Short Story Collections:
Like Birds, Like Fishes, 1964
A Stronger Climate, 1968
An Experience in India, 1970
How I Became a Holy Mother, 1976
Out of India (selected stories), 1986

Screenplays:
The Householder, 1963
Shakespeare Wallah, 1965
The Guru, 1968

Bombay Talkie, 1971

Autobiography of a Princess, 1975

Roseland, 1977

Hullabaloo Over Georgie and Bonnie's Picture, 1978

Jane Austen in Manhattan, 1980

Quartet, 1981

Heat and Dust, 1983

The Bostonians, 1984

A Room with a View, 1986
  (Academy Award, Best Screenplay)

Mr. & Mrs. Bridge, 1990

Howard's End, 1992
  (Academy Award, Best Adapted Screenplay)

The Remains of the Day, 1993
  (Academy Award nominee)

Jefferson in Paris, 1995

Writers Guild of America Honors:

A Room with a View, Best Screenplay, 1982

Howard's End, Nominee, Best Adapted Screenplay, 1992

Remains of the Day, Nominee, Best Adapted Screenplay, 1993

Foundation Career Achievement Award, 1995

Additional Honors:

Booker Award for Best Novel, 1995

Guggenheim Fellow, 1976

Nell Gunn International Fellow, 1976

MacArthur Fellow, 1984–89

A Screenwriter's Worst Nightmares

An Interview with

Laurence Dworet

"The real writers of movies are the executives who have the power to hire and fire and make sure they get the movie their way."
—Dr. Laurence Dworet

In the movie business, timing is often everything. Case in point: In 1981 Laurence Dworet, a young UCLA screenwriting student, appeared in my UCLA office asking permission to be accepted into my graduate screenwriting seminar. He did not introduce himself as Dr. Dworet nor did he mention that he was an emergency-room surgeon. He handed me a partially completed screenplay titled *Code Blue* as his ticket for admission, merely stating his intention to become a screenwriter. (The story of the beginning of Dr. Dworet's striving to become a screenwriter is told by him in *The New Screenwriter Looks at the New Screenwriter*, published by Silman-James in 1992.)

Though incomplete, the script had the beginnings of an outstanding piece of work—wonderfully written, suspenseful, thoroughly professional. I could not put it down. It could only have been written by someone with an extraordinary understanding and knowledge of emergency-room medicine. It was so authentic that you could hear the gurneys rushing down the hospital corridors, you could smell the disinfectant, the blood; feel the urgency as doctors and nurses fought frantically to save the lives of desperately ill and injured patients. And it went behind the scenes to tell a most unusual story of nationwide corruption inside the operation of ER units, which are owned by mega-corporations and apparently franchised (like KFC outlets).

Code Blue went on to win young Dr. Dworet the highly prized Samuel Goldwyn Award for best screenplay by a UCLA student, and with it always comes agents, job interviews, and all the good stuff young screenwriters long for.

As I write this, thirteen years after Laury wrote his story of an emergency-room surgeon, two of the most popular new series on television are *ER* and *Chicago Hope*, both about emergency-room medicine. Laury's superb script was more than a decade premature, an idea born thirteen years before it time.

Although *Code Blue* won young Dr. Dworet some serious attention no studio would touch it; "too realistic, too gory" were some of the comments. Television had been awash in such saccharine-soaked medical series as *Westside Medical* (I wrote one of those myself), *Dr. Kildare*, *Marcus Welby M.D.*, *Ben Casey* (the most realistic of the bunch), and others of that ilk, in which doctors, young or old, were all kindly know-it-alls, unerring in their judgment, and only sympathetic people fell ill and even fewer died. And because of the plethora of the TV doctor series, feature films wouldn't touch the subject. The same is true today.

It is likely that the runaway success of the all-time hit comedy series M*A*S*H (emergency-room medicine played for laughs) paved the way for the serious scalpels and suturing of *ER* and *Chicago Hope*.

But, times change. Not even the Republican Party can stop it. Television drama series have become much more realistic, hard-hitting, and true to life. Art not only imitates life but it is often the precursor of life. Once again, Dr. Dworet was on the cutting edge (pun unavoidable) with his screenplay of deadly viruses coming out of the rain forests, which he called *Outbreak*. The movie was less than a triumph, but it achieved those three hallowed words that are the be-all and end-all in Hollywood: It got made.

The story of the making of Laurence Dworet's first produced screenplay is, in itself, a movie, a horror story that is instructive for every aspiring screenwriter who ever fantasized about becoming a big-time, big-money screenwriter in the dream-factory town known as Hollywood.

However, Dr. Dworet's dream is a screenwriter's worst nightmare come true. Wannabe screenwriters beware! This tale is not for the squeamish.

FROUG: We really haven't talked about your career since four years ago when you sold your original screenplay *Ultimatum* to Disney for $500,000. Whatever happened to *Ultimatum*?

DWORET: It went through a wide variety of twists and turns. When they bought it, Jeffrey Katzenberg, then second-in-command at Disney, assured us that we'd be on the fast track and it would go into production quickly. And it seemed like it was going that route for the first month or so. They told us that they had so few notes on the screenplay that it was almost unheard of and that they would defer even giving us their notes until we had a director on board. So we had a meeting with the director and with one of the chief executives in a room with over forty other people. Then one exec said, "Gee, I see this script very differently than the way it's written. I think it needs a lot more romance and sex." Nobody said a word, and I was very naive about how you're supposed to behave in these meetings. I'm very frank with my patients—in the world of medicine you don't beat around the bush. So I said, "Listen, the guy has forty-eight hours to find a nuclear bomb. How many times can he fuck his girlfriend?" [Laughter] Everybody laughed. The executive turned beet red, and decided that the script would go forward just the way it was. Then Steven Spielberg got hold of the script through Warren Beatty. We were told that Spielberg's reaction was, "This is the greatest script I've read in three years. Why wasn't I shown this project?" Well, he wasn't shown the project for a variety of reasons, one of them being that we didn't want to get into a situation where Spielberg had to decide what he wanted to do, which could take a lot of time. And that's exactly what happened. He basically took over the project, wresting it from Disney. And right after he said this was the greatest script in three years, he wouldn't even meet with us. We were summarily fired.

FROUG: Without a meeting?

DWORET: Without even a meeting. We were told that Spielberg wanted someone with whom he had a shorthand, someone who would know quickly what he wanted. Wesley Strick was that writer of the moment for Spielberg, so Strick was going to come in and do it. But six months later, Spielberg changed his mind: He just wasn't sure what he wanted to do. So Disney finally got the screenplay back. Then, the executive who had wanted to turn it into a sex movie finally had his opportunity. He hired two famous writers—a husband and wife team, both novelists. They spent three weeks on the beach in Hawaii rewriting the script completely. They were supposed to stick to our structure. But not a word was the same. Their rewrite was so bad that the executive himself had to bury it in a drawer. He then hired four writers for fantastic sums of money and got a journeyman director that he could control completely. The script went through all these permutations, from a suspense melodrama to a Bruce Willis action-comedy to a sex movie.

FROUG: *Ultimatum* was basically a story about terrorists who had hidden a nuclear bomb somewhere in New York City, right?

DWORET: They hid it somewhere and the authorities had two days to find it. We know these terrorists are real because, in the middle of the movie, they explode a nuclear bomb in a rural area of the United States.

FROUG: To show that they know how to do it?

DWORET: Yeah, to show that this is what's coming next, and it could be in a city where millions of people are going to die. It's very suspenseful. Every studio in town wanted to buy it at the time, but it never did get made. The good news is that the 1988 Writers Guild agreement on original material was, thank God, applicable here. It stipulates that five years after the original writer's last work on a screenplay, it reverts back to him for the sum of money he was paid, plus interest. If the movie goes into production, you have to pay the other writers, but you don't have to pay the producing fees, which are substantial in this case. It's bad enough that the writing fees will be over two and a half million, but at least there is not another one and a half million or whatever in producing and directing fees and all that.

FROUG: So the script has now reverted to you?

DWORET: It's going to revert to me and Robert Pool on October 20.

FROUG: What do you think the chances are of selling it with that price tag on it?

DWORET: Well, it's $500,000 up front. It could be developed for that, and an executive at Fox has already told me that he wants it badly.

FROUG: Let's go to *Outbreak*. Did it share a similar fate?

DWORET: It was quite different. I was hired to do *Outbreak* on the basis of: "We want you to write a story about viruses because we think the subject of viruses is going to be hot."

FROUG: This is because of the *New Yorker* article?

DWORET: The *New Yorker* article called *The Hot Zone* got all the studios hot about viruses.

FROUG: *The Hot Zone* was not fictional.

DWORET: It was a factual account of a number of outbreaks of the Ebola and other viruses. Seemingly, by man infringing upon the rain forest and our delicate ecosystems, we're exposing ourselves to these horrendously virulent viruses. And it's only a matter of time before one hits Western civilization. So Bob Pool and I were brought in.

FROUG: This was when you were a team?

DWORET: We were a team then; we no longer are. I looked at the material and said, "This isn't the movie I want to make. I don't want to buy the rights to the article because there's nothing in it that I need."

FROUG: Were you still working as a part-time emergency-room surgeon?

DWORET: Almost full-time. What I wanted to write was a movie that would scare me as an emergency-room doctor—something about my experiences, what I worry about, and all these terrible diseases that my very poorest patients often bring in because they come from God-knows-what country where they haven't had any medical care. They expose me and my staff to these terrible diseases, which I worry about getting and transmitting to my family. I told the studio executives that a story like that scares me, and it's the only one I would want to write. They said that it sounded great; we were in synch. At that time, I didn't have a human villain—our virus was the villain. Ironically, much of the criticism of *Outbreak* has been from critics who wondered why the filmmakers anthropomorphized the villain when they had such an incredible villain of nature.

FROUG: There were a lot of critics who thought the Donald Sutherland character was way overboard.

DWORET: Right. Why do we need a human villain when we have a spreading virus that's wiping out humanity?

FROUG: Whose notion was the human villain, the studio's?

DWORET: The studio executives', yeah.

FROUG: Tell me, do these guys all get together and work as a committee to decide how to screw up the script?

DWORET: Well, I think there are certain formulas they look for that are familiar. You have to put yourself in the position of the executives. Somerset Maugham said that you have to have compassion for everyone. I certainly try to, especially when it comes to studio executives. These guys have to support a family. They're in a very competitive field; 100 guys want those positions and their jobs are on the line every minute. They don't want to make a mistake, and they never want to be pinned with responsibility for anything that isn't incredibly successful. As a result, they only feel safe by going to formula all the time. I think that because I was a doctor and because there was this race to do a virus story, they pretty much gave

"Somerset Maugham said that you have to have compassion for everyone. I certainly try to, especially when it comes to studio executives."

me carte blanche—I could do whatever I wanted—at least on the first draft. I even killed off the hero.

FROUG: The hero who became the Dustin Hoffman character?

DWORET: The hero was always the same guy, but he was a real son of a bitch. He was a Patton-like figure, a man who had a real clear character arc and a real need to succeed, a guy who was, like many doctors I know, great to his patients, great in terms of his research and stuff, but a real son of a bitch to be around. And only by dealing with the virus and getting infected by the virus was he humanized in a certain sense.

FROUG: Which is a hell of a good story by itself.

DWORET: It's a great story. I finished three drafts along those lines: where doctors made mistakes and this arrogant son of a bitch made mistakes that he had to live with, which was a hard thing for him to do. When I finished the third draft, everybody liked it except one executive, who said, "No, we just came out with *The Fugitive*, which is going to be a rip-roaring hit. We want you to turn the movie into a medical-*Fugitive*, virus-*Fugitive* type of a thing. I was thoroughly pissed off. It was clear that they wouldn't go any other way. I said, "This is the stupidest idea," and I quit and went off to Europe for the summer with my family. When I came back, I said, "If you let me do it my way, I'll take one shot at a thriller." My partner had made one attempt that they had rejected. It wasn't at all what they wanted, so they said to just throw all that out and start from scratch. I said that I already had, and I threw a story at them, which they liked very much. Three weeks later, when I went back to tweak a few things in the third act, the executive said to me, "Throw the entire thing out—the whole idea, the whole story." I said, "But only last month, you loved the first two acts." He said, "Let's just throw the whole thing out." I said, "That's enough, I'm finished, I've got another project at the studio, I'm moving on." And for a few weeks, I quit the project. Then I spoke to Arnold Kopelson, the producer, and his people. They said, "Look, we'll keep this guy out of your hair; we don't want to lose this race to Fox. Just do it your way, the way you wanted to do it when you came back from Europe, and nobody's going to bother you." Well, luckily Kopelson loved that script. It was a real kick-ass action script, and it had a good villain—it had the Morgan Freeman character as the main villain—no cartoon villain in it. The Donald Sutherland character hardly existed. It was about this guy, the Freeman character, who's morally torn between trying to preserve his program and trying to do the right thing. He is a decent guy, a villain you understand. And there is a great moment where he has to choose between his top-secret viral research and destroying the entire town. You feel his pain, you feel his decision that put him in this position where the virus is really going to spread out of that town, not just that map on the wall in the movie that turns all red. In the movie, I never felt the virus was going to spread out of the town. But in my script, it was very clear because I spent the whole third act showing how it was getting worse and spreading to the water table and all these things to really drum up the action so that the Morgan Freeman character would have the difficult decision that if he didn't destroy that town, he would be literally exposing the whole world to this virus. It was a decision that I felt that if I had to make, I would probably destroy the town and kill all those people.

FROUG: Well, that's a hell of a good moral dilemma. That's got a great core conflict to it. But they threw out everything?

DWORET: They threw it all out. They brought in Ted Tally, who won the Academy Award for his adaptation of *Silence of the Lambs*. He basically kept the exact same structure and all the characters, but working together with the director, came up with that cartoon villain, the Donald Sutherland character, which was so stupid that I couldn't conceive that Tally could write it. There was no way to write it well because it was just dumb from the beginning.

FROUG: Is Tally one of those guys they're paying $100,000 a week to do rewrites?

DWORET: He got half a million dollars for the revision. As a writer, he tried his best, and he came up with some good stuff. He pumped up some of the dialogue, he made some of the director's changes, but basically, not a single scene changed. And after Tally's draft, Hoffman came in with Carrie Fisher to redo his dialogue. She would submit a stack of handwritten pages and, so I've heard, basically say, "Just take whatever of them you want."

FROUG: What did they pay her?

DWORET: She got, I think, about a quarter of a million dollars.

FROUG: Now Tally, at this point, got about a half a million.

DWORET: He'd gotten a half a million, but he quit suddenly and then we were called back. I couldn't go back because I was in the middle of *Young Men and Fire*. The producer hadn't been pleased with part of it; I said, "Let's get it right," and stayed on that project. So they brought in Jeb Stuart because he had done *The Fugitive*, and they felt he could fix anything.

FROUG: He could make *Outbreak* into *The Fugitive*, right?

DWORET: That's what they thought. Anyway, he came up with some scheme that just didn't work. He wrote a draft a week for four weeks, and at the end of those four weeks the script was, in my opinion, just awful.

FROUG: How much did he get paid?

DWORET: A half a million dollars for about five weeks. At this point, the director was thoroughly dispirited and went back to the Tally draft and my draft. The Tally draft was all my structure and my scenes and they started shooting that. You have to remember that, at this point, Fox was supposed to start a virus movie as well. They'd already poured eight million dollars into it.

FROUG: Into *The Hot Zone*?

DWORET: Right. And then it fell apart.

FROUG: Robert Redford was in it and pulled out?

DWORET: Jodie Foster had already pulled out because there were some problems with the script. They simply couldn't make a story out of that article; it never would work. What they ended up doing was drifting more and more toward my movie, which featured a disease affecting humans, which in the book was just confined to monkeys. Eventually, the disease in *The Hot Zone* script spreads to humans.

FROUG: So it became your script.

DWORET: More and more it became my script and, you know, I thought this was quite funny. But when the Fox project was stalled, the situation with *Outbreak* changed dramatically. Until then, Dustin Hoffman supposedly had been doing a really good job of just making the movie. But now, with the winner of the race no longer in question, he wanted to change the whole script.

FROUG: While you're shooting?

DWORET: Well, they stopped production for a week so they could "fix the script" or whatever. They brought in Neal Jimenez to do dialogue changes for $60,000 a week.

FROUG: He's a very good writer.

DWORET: Good writer, but somehow, in this case, this wasn't the kind of material he knew. They ended up improvising the dialogue on the set, hardly using any of his material.

FROUG: This is Hoffman and the others?

DWORET: And the others. The producer said they often would get a fax at four in the morning saying what the scene would be for that morning. Often they didn't even know what the scene was going to be. It was completely chaotic. Whereas all they had to do was shoot the draft that Tally had written and it would have worked fine.

FROUG: Hoffman being Hoffman?

DWORET: Exactly. He later claimed, in an article I read, that he made up sixty to seventy percent of the script, which is ridiculous. All the tensions of the scenes were the same. They did make up the dialogue, but one of the reasons they made up the dialogue was because it was so flat. They had to keep improvising it because they were changing it so much that they lost contact with the original script.

FROUG: At this point, is Neal Jimenez doing it or is Carrie Fisher doing it?

DWORET: Jimenez is on the set at this point. He was on the set for nineteen weeks.

FROUG: So he's got over a million dollars now for rewrites?

DWORET: Right, he got roughly a million. And then, at the same time that Jimenez is on the set, they bring in Rene Russo's husband, Dan Gilroy. He was one of the writers of *Freejack*. Wolfgang told us he likes to have a writer on the set all the time. He wanted us on the set. When we said no, he got Jeb Stuart and Neal Jimenez and then Dan Gilroy at the end, when they seemingly didn't have an ending. They kept changing their minds. They literally didn't know what the end of the movie was. When I saw the first cut, the last third was horrendous. I couldn't follow it. And I had conceived the story! Eventually, they had to reshoot much of the end. They even brought in Maya Angelou to basically redo the ending of the movie and write some of Dustin's dialogue. They also brought in Patrick Caddell, the pollster, to write that White House scene.

FROUG: My God. This is incredible!

DWORET: They also had lines of dialogue coming from the production assistants on the set. Utter chaos.

FROUG: The interesting thing about this, Laury, as far as I can see, is that in spite of these millions and millions of dollars going to rewriters and rewriters of rewriters and more rewriters, when you get all done, the Writers Guild, as we both know, determines credits on all movies. They examine everything that's been written in connection with the movie—every word, every line, from the very first sentence put on paper, is read by an arbitration committee of three screenwriters. And the committee decided that you and Bob Pool still ended up with the only writing credits.

DWORET: Yes, because Jimenez changed what we calculated to be no more than eleven percent. You can't give a guy credit for changing the dialogue if the intention of every line is almost the same.

FROUG: I've been a member of several of those WGA arbitration committees; to earn a credit, the changes made by subsequent writers must be significant.

DWORET: All they did was change some words. They kept my structure. The first ninety minutes of the movie followed that structure almost completely. In the last thirty minutes, they also followed it, but unfortunately left too much of it out. They changed the villain, and toward the end, it wasn't nearly as strong as the first ninety minutes.

FROUG: Is all this chaos just desperation on everybody's part to get a hit?

DWORET: I think it comes from not knowing what to do. It's insecurity that creates chaos once you start monkeying with something that worked and writing by committee. How can you satisfy all these people?

"It's insecurity that creates chaos once you start monkeying with something that worked and writing by committee."

FROUG: Now that you've gone through this insane experience, does it make you want to rush back to medicine and say to hell with screenwriting?

DWORET: Well, you know, there is chaos in medicine now that really rivals or exceeds the chaos in that movie.

FROUG: How can it be more chaotic than Hollywood?

DWORET: Because doctors have to deal with the HMO revolution that is overtaking American medicine, and the politics in medicine today are just awful. It's very hard to do what's best for your patient because you've got everybody looking over your shoulder. The hospital administrators are trying to cut your costs—you have to order fewer and fewer tests. You have the patients and their lawyers, and if, God forbid, you ever make a mistake in the emergency room, they're going to come after you because you never see the patient again; you never have a chance to develop any doctor-patient rapport. It's an extremely tricky situation. But, you know, I like writing now. This is the first time I've had a chance to write for a year without having to work as a doctor. I wrote *Young Men in Fire*. I was very pleased with it. And I was able to get it to a bunch of directors who wanted to do it.

FROUG: As a screenwriter, what do you do to prevent the same thing that has happened on everything you've done from happening all over again on *Young Men in Fire*? Have you ever had a movie where your script was shot and that's it?

DWORET: No. *Outbreak* is the first movie I've had produced, even though I've been very close on many others.

FROUG: But you've sold a lot of scripts.

DWORET: I've sold a lot of screenplays. The first one was *The Practice* back in '84. It was going to get produced and at the last second it didn't. The director came in and started changing the script, which I thought really mucked it up, really destroyed it.

FROUG: Let's talk about *Code Blue*, which you did when you were my student. It was twelve to fifteen years ahead of its time. The idea of an emergency-room operating theater for the core of the drama was new, and now there are two emergency-room dramas on television.

DWORET: It was ahead of its time. And I'd written a script seven or eight years ago about computers and the lack of privacy. And then a nuclear thriller. Now there are many computer movies out there, but I couldn't sell mine seven or eight years ago. It was just too far ahead of its time. And it was the same with the nuclear thriller. Back in 1981, people said, "It's not going to happen. We don't want to make this movie."

FROUG: So the subject matters you picked were ahead of their time?

DWORET: A lot of it is the subject matter, which has to be something that really excites you.

FROUG: How do you pick a subject matter that hasn't been done, or isn't too far ahead of it's time? Ideas get in the air, don't you think? Like, "Let's do a virus movie"?

DWORET: We were ahead of the curve there with the other studio. To be honest, there have been a dozen other virus movies made over the last fifteen to twenty years. Most of them had to do with military conspiracies, which is the reason that,

"This executive had it in his mind, from the very first meeting, that this would become a military, biological thriller because he was interested in conspiracies. He sees the world through a different lens than some of us."

when I first came to the project, I said that I'm not doing a military–conspiracy virus movie. It's stupid.

FROUG: That's exactly what they turned it into.

DWORET: Exactly. This executive had it in his mind, from the very first meeting, that this would become a military, biological thriller because he was interested in conspiracies. He sees the world through a different lens than some of us. This was his idea from the very beginning, and he turned the movie around to fit his idea.

FROUG: Just like the executive at Disney who tried to turn your nuclear thriller, *Ultimatum*, into a sex movie?

DWORET: Yeah. At some level, the real writers of movies are the executives who have the power to hire and fire and make sure they get the movie their way.

FROUG: I know you're right about their jobs being on the line, but doesn't common sense set in at some point? Are they beyond that?

DWORET: I think it's their insecurity and their power. When you combine insecurity and power, you have a very unpredictable course, and it's certainly never going to be what you first went in with. I think you have to accept that. I think that's what writers have to deal with. I hope to have a much stronger turnaround clause in all my contracts, so that if the script isn't going to be made, I can get it back. Even if they just like the germ of an idea I come up with, they clearly have the power to do anything they want with it. That's the way the game is played, and you have to accept that when you get on the field. Otherwise, you look for HBO movies; you look for cable movies; you look for independently financed movies, which someday I'm going to consider.

FROUG: The rare case, for example, is Eric Roth, who told me *Forrest Gump* was shot almost exactly the way he wrote it. Almost unheard of.

DWORET: And I just worked with a director developing *Young Men in Fire*. My input was really appreciated. I had the final word on what could be written, but there were certain twists and turns in the development that went the way of the director. I knew it was going to be his way, no matter what. And so you may say that, yes, you're the only writer, but you know that certain things are being changed for the better, and maybe not for the better. Since filmmaking is a collaborative art, you have to see it as some kind of compromise, and find the best compromise possible.

FROUG: You packed up your family and moved to Santa Barbara about a year ago. Is it easier to work from that distance or is it more difficult?

DWORET: I think that, as a producer, you have to be in town. The meetings and the deals and so much depend on friends of the moment whom you're kind of in bed with, sometimes literally. But as a writer, I'm only ninety minutes away. I never was one for taking meetings. I had friends who always took meetings that never did anything to enhance their careers. I felt that if they had spent their time writing rather than taking meetings, they would be far better writers. It's only the quality of the work that gets you the job. It's a fallacy to think that your agent gets you work. I've never had an agent get me

"Since filmmaking is a collaborative art, you have to see it as some kind of compromise, and find the best compromise possible."

a job, and I don't expect it. The agent is there to make the best deal for you. The agent is someone who can give you advice. When I lived in Hollywood, I hated the fact that everybody I knew bitched and moaned about their agent. Thank God, I don't have to listen to that anymore up here, because there's nobody here. Well, there are people in the business, but very few of them. The key is for your agent to be your consultant, somebody who can give you good advice, somebody who can make the best deal possible for you and keep you out of trouble. You have to be able to manage your own career.

FROUG: How do you like working alone now, as opposed to working with a partner? What's the difference?

DWORET: Somewhere in the middle of *Outbreak*, Bob Pool and I split up because we had different sensibilities. We had split up before, back in '84, and later he had a movie made, *Big Town*, which was a great honor.

FROUG: Did it go anywhere?

DWORET: No, it didn't. But there was something wonderful he told me: Bob said that there was his movie, it was up on the screen, faithful to his script. I think the best thing about working alone is that you get to follow your own vision, follow your own sensibility. The characters are just coming out of you. I've had good relationships with writing partners. I like to write alone and I like to write with a partner if the chemistry is really right. Sometimes it's wonderful to sit in a room and work out scenes together. It's not as fast as writing by yourself. Is it as good? Sometimes it's very good. Sometimes it's a lot of fun. There's that loneliness. I hate the

solitariness of being a writer. The emergency room is wonderful in the sense that it is reality. Writing is utter fantasy. I
need that balance. Balance is important to my life. After four
or five days of writing, just being all alone in a room, I used
to go to the ER and see sixty patients in a day. I'd be the
general of my own army, if you will, as an ER doctor.

FROUG: Nobody is rewriting you?

DWORET: Right. You've got immediate gratification because you
walk in the door and you save somebody's life. Gratification in
the movie business is very slow in coming. If it ever comes.
The only reason that *Outbreak* got made was because of the
competition with Fox. If there wasn't that competition,
Outbreak would have been in "Development Hell."

FROUG: Will they ever get even with it?

DWORET: I don't know.

FROUG: It's about a forty- or fifty-million-dollar picture, isn't it?

DWORET: As it turns out, the movie was actually the number-one
box-office hit from January 1st through May 31st. It made
about sixty-five million, which put it in the number-one slot
for all movies released this year. It's going to be exceeded, but
for those five months it was the number-one movie and that
was just U.S. It's already done far more in the foreign market
than it did in he U.S. It's going through the roof. So they're
gonna easily get their money back.

FROUG: But will it ever show a profit on the studio books?

DWORET: Well, given that *Forrest Gump* doesn't show a profit, I
don't expect that *Outbreak* ever will either. You have a gross-
profits player like Dustin Hoffman taking money off the top.

He'll see a lot of money, but there won't be any net profits for the rest of us.

FROUG: Do you have a piece of the net, the writer's usual five "points," as they call percentages in Hollywood?

DWORET: Yeah, but I've never seen it and nobody else that I know of ever has either.

FROUG: No writer I have ever known has ever seen anything of that five-percent net. Do you think it's a myth?

DWORET: Yeah. Anybody who's been in town for business for any length of time doesn't ever expect it. But I enjoyed the virus movie, anyway. To me it was an accomplishment. I like writing.

FROUG: Like most writers I know, you seem to have a love/hate relationship with writing.

DWORET: I've always been fortunate being an ER doctor, having another profession to fall back on, so I could write what I wanted to write. And now it's funny, I sit in a room all day—from eight to five—which is great, I love to sit in the room and write. And it's hard to believe that somebody pays me to sit here, dreaming and thinking. I also felt the same when I was a practicing doctor. I was unbelievably lucky to be doing something that I would've done for free because it was so much fun. I count myself unbelievably lucky to have a couple of jobs that, you know, you die for. What can be more important than an emergency-room doctor? And there couldn't be anything more creative than being a screenwriter, at least when you're doing your own thing and not what somebody's telling you to do.

" . . . it's hard to believe that somebody pays me to sit here, dreaming and thinking. I also felt the same when I was a practicing doctor. I was unbelievably lucky to be doing something that I would've done for free because it was so much fun."

FROUG: That's rare, isn't it?

DWORET: It is rare, but at some point, with the scripts I write, I mostly do my own thing. I don't know how long I can continue doing it. I took two studio jobs at Warner Bros. One of them got made, but the other one is going to be a long haul, even though there's been a lot of interest in it.

FROUG: This is *Young Men in Fire*?

DWORET: Yes. It's a different kind of movie. It's more akin to Redford's *A River Runs Through It*, which was completely independently financed, made before the studio had any interest in it. I know it wasn't a perfect movie, but he made it his way. It's his vision of the movie, and it's a unified vision, whether it works or not. I found some of it very slow, personally. But nobody told him to add a lot of action and sex to it.

FROUG: Are you thinking about going back to being a part-time doctor?

DWORET: Not yet. Not for a few years, actually.

FROUG: Do you work at home?

DWORET: I leave the house around eight A.M. and work in my office from eight to about five.

FROUG: Where's your office?

DWORET: Downtown Santa Barbara. I can write undisturbed. Nobody has my phone number. The key thing is cutting out the phone calls. I don't even have a phone in my room. I don't take any calls, ever. And sometimes I write twelve or fourteen hours a day. When I was under the gun on *Outbreak*,

"If I think of a scene that I really like, I figure out how I can work up to that scene and down from that scene. The most creative part of the movie, to me, is not just coming up with the characters, it's the story process."

there was so much pressure to get it done, I had very little time to do an entirely new draft from start to finish. It was a completely different movie than I had written before, and I had to get it done in about eight weeks. It was a little bit rough. There was more work that I wanted to do on it, but I didn't want to fight any more battles with the executive.

FROUG: Do you make an outline before you start writing?

DWORET: I do, but I try to keep it very fluid. It's like when Walter Newman came to class one day and said, "I write down all my ideas. I use index cards and then I shuffle them and I juggle them." I keep it very free. If I think of a scene that I really like, I figure out how I can work up to that scene and down from that scene. The most creative part of the movie, to me, is not just coming up with the characters, it's the story process. I create this story in a very free-form way.

FROUG: As you're going along?

DWORET: No, I don't do it as I'm writing the script. I make up the story from the characters without writing the whole scene. I'll write a few lines and then, maybe, the beat of the scene. If I don't do the story first, but just write, I often find that I get about forty pages in and there aren't enough twists and turns, there aren't enough surprises, in the script. I'd rather take the time up front to sit there thinking and creating: What would this character do at this moment? It's not that I don't change significantly when I'm writing the script, because even then I like to have something that I haven't thought of. In other words, I have to know where I'm going in the script. It's not rigid. I'll take it in different directions. But, for me, having the step-outline somehow works better.

FROUG: It's worked for you so far. And I think you're going to find it'll be working better and better as you get more credits piled up, and they begin to feel that you can write a money-making movie. Do you think that they then will begin to back off?

DWORET: Yeah, I think so. I think the success of *Outbreak* has kept the producers at bay when I say, "Look, I know what works." Everything in *Outbreak* that worked in terms of the structure worked because I felt it worked. One of the strengths that they recognized in me was my sense of structure. I seem to be good at that. I count my blessings, because structure is something I've been very strong at since I was kid—something about storytelling and making it exciting and avoiding being bored. You're always looking for something you've never seen before. Or at least some twist or turn and, you know, as you said in class, "Never do it if you've seen it before. Never do the same thing, and keep information to a minimum"—a lot of the basic things that you taught us long ago and Walter Newman reiterated.

FROUG: Walter Newman was my mentor. Walter was a master.

DWORET: Walter was a master. Some of those most basic things are what makes the difference between an exciting movie and a boring movie. A more exciting story, I should say. Even in the story phase, those are the key things. There are so many opportunities to go wrong in writing a script. You have to find the right path.

FROUG: And to have the imagination and intuition to know what works.

DWORET: Yes. A lot of that is, of course, seeing many movies. I've seen I-don't-know-how-many thousands of movies. It's all part of the process of becoming a screenwriter.

CREDITS

Berlin Blues, 1989 (shared credit)
Outbreak, 1995 (shared credit)
Young Men and Fire
Ultimatum

Mind in its purest play is like some bat
That beats about in caverns all alone,
Contriving by some sort of senseless wit
Not to conclude against a wall of stone.
—Richard Wilbur, *Mind*

Persons attempting to find a motive in this narrative
will be prosecuted; persons attempting to find a moral
in it will be banished; persons attempting to find a plot
in it will be shot.
—Mark Twain, *The Adventures of Huckleberry Finn*

You write a hit play the same way you write a flop.
—William Saroyan

Hunting Big Game

How do you know your screenplay will sell? How do you get an agent, win recognition, get writing jobs, earn professional status? These are tough questions.

You can never be sure your screenplay will sell, but you can never be sure it won't. Hollywood is essentially a whimsical town. Since there is no certainty of success, most of the movers and shakers, even after extensive market research (which experience tells them is often wrong), tend to go with their hunches. Gradually, as the necessary enthusiasm builds to support a hunch, other movers and shakers jump on the bandwagon. Hence, the almost routine coincidence of several studios and/or networks developing the same subject matter at the same time. If one network is doing an emergency-hospital series, "we'll do it, too, only better," is the way the thinking generally goes. If some studio is planning a *King Kong* remake, another studio is probably doing so, too. How many films did my buddy the late Gene Roddenberry's *Star Trek* inspire? Knock-offs have a long history, not only in filmmaking, but in publishing, fashion, and every corner of capitalism.

"Nothing succeeds like excess," as Larry Gelbart has remarked. If one lawyer series works, how about two or three? One dysfunctional family sitcom is a hit, how about a dozen more? Imitation is not the sincerest form of flattery, it's the sincerest form of desperation.

The only conclusion you can logically draw from the flood of crap on the tube and on the movie scene is that there just isn't enough top-level material to go around. And that's the blunt truth of it.

How many great doctors are there, great leaders, great teachers, great poets, novelists, painters, screenwriters, movies? Think about it. The reason there's always room at the top is that there are so few people up there. Whereas mediocrity is a mob scene. What is it the sage said? God must have loved the mediocre because he made so many of us? Great artists, great scientists, great anythings are rarities.

If you even suspect you have what it takes to produce something of very high quality (which, these days, is often merely above the norm), there is a desperately hungry army of buyers eager to see or read your material. This does not, of course, mean you are guaranteed success. But it does guarantee you *access* to the marketplace. Exciting new talent is always in demand. The town is desperately hoping for somebody or something to get excited about. It's the juice that keeps the film world's adrenaline pumping. When a hot new screenwriter hits town, the town lights up. Everybody wants to get in on the action. The same is true for a hot new director, actor, whatever.

But the screenwriter has a big advantage over the actor and the director. Actors have to go somewhere to be seen; they have to perform in local theaters, have to be seen by key people (agents, execs, producers, et al.), and, unless they are the studio head's wife, they must travel a long, tough road just to become qualified for professional auditions. Directors have it even tougher. They have to find the money to make a small film to demonstrate their work. Screenwriters, on the other hand, can sit at home with pad and pencil, typewriter, word processor, or whatever tool they choose and put their words on paper. What other film artist has it better than that?

· · · · ·

When you do finally put your work before the powers that be, submit only your best work. Never submit something about which you have serious reservations. If you're uncertain about your script, give it to a select few friends (not relatives, who will probably heap only flattery on you). Choose friends who are movie buffs, who are knowledgeable, who can discuss your screenplay in reference to other films they've seen. Feedback is important, especially at the beginning of your career.

Of course, there's nothing better than starting at the top of your profession. However, with screenwriters, this happens to only the gifted few or those who are willing to devote themselves whole-heartedly to developing the talent they have by writing screenplay after screenplay. For all the books on screenwriting (including mine), for all the gurus and their lectures on structure, nothing and nobody can teach you screenwriting as well as you can teach yourself, *learning by doing.*

Batter Up!

I was one of the eleven founding members of the Caucus for Producers, Writers, and Directors in Hollywood, a group of primarily writer-producer hyphenates who decided we needed an organization to represent us against management. The Writers Guild could not legally represent us since we were also supervisors. The Producers Guild of America, of which I was a member of the board of directors for twelve or thirteen years, also could not represent us for the same reason: Employees who are supervisors are not allowed labor representation, regardless of the fact that they are non-management, salaried employees.

In forming the Caucus, we asked a few dozen of the top writer-producer-directors to join with us. In short order, we had 200 of the best in the business. I was elected to the Steering Committee and remained a member of it for twelve years, later becoming Chairman.

In my ongoing relationship with our membership, I learned a valuable lesson: Nobody who creates television programs deliberately produces down to the lowest common denominator; nobody says, in advance, "This is trash, but I think I can get the public to buy it." Similarly, I never met a program creator who was certain about what would be popular or what would not be popular. It's a guessing game and everybody in motion pictures and television has to play it every day of their lives. William Goldman put it accurately and succinctly in his superb analysis of Hollywood filmmaking, *Adventures in the Screen Trade*. He said, when it comes to knowing what an audience will pay to see, "Nobody Knows Anything."

The Golden Guts

Everybody in our field created shows that they themselves enjoyed. In many cases, what the show's creator liked, the public liked; in just as many cases, they didn't. *I learned early on that the big winners were always the exceptionally talented men or women who wrote or produced shows they, themselves, really enjoyed.*

One of my fellow Caucus-founding members was Aaron Spelling, whose uncanny ability to make television series of mass popularity for several decades now has reportedly put him in the billionaire class. (His hit series include the current *Melrose Place* and *Beverly Hills 90210.*) There hasn't been a TV season without an Aaron Spelling hit in many years. At one time, it was said he practically owned the ABC network; and his exclusive contract kept them afloat during their fledgling years.

I know Aaron well enough to know that he doesn't produce down to the audience. He produces shows he likes and, as it happens, so do many millions of other people. This talent is known as having a golden gut.

Another of our founding members was Norman Lear, another possible candidate for billionaire status except for his exceptional sense of social responsibility. (Norman is famous for donating "seed money" to establish worthwhile programs.)

Unlike Aaron, Norman's tastes have always been daring, out of the mainstream. He produced (with his then partner, Bud Yorkin) the classic *All in the Family*, then *Maude*, then *Sanford and Son*, followed by *The Jeffersons* (the latter two being among the first African-American sitcoms). Norman has always been a man of exceptional courage as well as societal concern, and his shows have reflected that.

Could anybody have guessed that his controversial, offbeat shows would consistently achieve the highest ratings in television? In a few words, Norman Lear is a daring, born leader and a super human being who has followed his own vision most of his life. And his golden gut is connected to a heart of pure gold.

As Spelling and Lear clearly demonstrate, you do not get fame or fortune from trying to second-guess the marketplace, which is a fool's game.

Going with Inflamed Golden Guts

As an example of the extent to which a dedicated screenwriter will go to pursue his dreams, I give you the extraordinary case of my friend and former student Dan O'Bannon. Dan inherited inflammatory bowel disease, which is both incurable and exceedingly painful. (Dan has spent a great deal of his life in and out of hospitals.) Undeterred since his earliest days as a USC screenwriting student,

Dan has sat before his keyboard, in agonizing pain, and pounded out winning screenplay after winning screenplay.

When I last watched Dan work, some years ago, he was seated at a small table in a nearly bare room with a thirty-five-gallon trash barrel beside him. He told me that since science-fiction movies had seemingly run their course, it was time for him to write one. He had an idea, unoutlined, and began to pound away, putting down a few words on a sheet of paper, crumpling it up angrily and tossing into the trash barrel, which was already overflowing. "I have this idea," he told me, "and I've got to write it, no matter what."

He did, writing through his pain, and sold it. It was called *Alien*. It made Dan O'Bannon a screenwriting star, and inspired two sequels, both of which earned him tidy royalties. No pain, no gain? Maybe, but the point is, if you write what you truly believe in, no matter what, you're a leg up on success. Dan's golden guts are racked with pain, but they don't deter him from following his very personal vision. He also went on to co-write *Blue Thunder*, *Total Recall*, and others.

The last time I saw Dan was when I interviewed him for *The New Screenwriter Looks at the New Screenwriter*. He at the UCLA Hospital, where, hooked up to an IV on a rolling stand, he paced the floor in his hospital gown and talked effusively about the new screenplay he was planing to write. That, my friends, is a nothing-will-stand-in-my-way screenwriter.

Dan understands that he must follow his vision, his instincts are his guide, and this holds true for all really successful screenwriters. They understand the first lesson: You, the writer, are the first audience you have to please. If you're lucky, maybe millions of other people all over the world will also be pleased. If you're not lucky, move on to your next project.

Audiences are begging for stories, eager to be informed and entertained. Step up to the plate and give it your best effort. The reverberations of one single hit might be heard all around the planet. It happens again and again.

Above all, follow your gut instincts.

Don't Call Me, and I Won't Call You

Once you determine you're going to be screenwriter, determine that you can handle rejection. If you commit yourself to any artistic career, you cannot avoid instances of being replaced by some fellow artist, dismissed, fired, rejected, or told to take a walk.

No matter how successful you become ("important" is Hollywood's favorite word), you will sometimes be told that your effort "just doesn't cut it," you will be fired off the picture and be replaced faster than a star phones his or her agent. The most popular comment that comes with the dismissal is "it's nothing personal."

Of course it's personal, and it burns like fire. You'll be angered, if not infuriated, but you must never ever let yourself be defeated. In the whimsical world of moviemaking, almost anything can set off a panic attack. Walk in one day with the wrong shoe color or wrong joke and you're history. Writers can easily conclude that they are as interchangeable as T-shirts. And sometimes the establishment thinks they are.

There is only one healthy response to this infuriating situation. Turn your energy away from anger and into the writing of a new screenplay—preferably one based on your own original story. If you write an original, no matter what happens, it's yours—you own it. They can fire you off the picture, they can humiliate you, but in the end, the first writer will always get a big piece of the credit, no matter how many writers are brought in to rewrite.

Replacing screenwriters is a popular blood sport in Hollywood. Studio executives, producers, directors, stars, or whoever has the most power on the particular project can and often does decide, "We need some fresh thinking, some new ideas." All of these characters seem to have a writer with whom they have a special level of communication (this month, that is), and they'll turn to that writer faster than they can drive their Mercedes down the San Diego Freeway. Of course, it's ridiculous, but you have to understand that these people have fifty- to one-hundred-million dollars riding on the project, and sometimes their jobs.

Desperation is the name of the game in Hollywood. The studios have painted themselves into a corner with outrageous star salaries and feature-film budgets. The script doesn't satisfy the director (or star)? Just throw another million dollars at it and your worries are over. At least, so goes the present Hollywood mindset.

The bodies of rejected screenwriters lie about the Hollywood landscape like so much chaff.

Actually, as hard as it is to believe, it really isn't personal. Write a great screenplay the next time around and they'll be fawning all over you. You'll be their best friend and your previous "sins" will be immediately forgotten. Screenwriters, like actors and directors, are just another commodity in the world of Hollywood moviemaking. Everybody who works in movieland gets hit with big-time rejection now and then. And the bigger they come, as the saying goes, the harder they fall.

Consider how Arnold Schwarzenegger must have felt after the audience and the critics beat him to a pulp on his megaflop *The Last Action Hero*. Mr. S. understood that the necessary response to making a flop is making a hit next time. A hit is the best revenge. So James Cameron came up with *True Lies*; Schwarzenegger grabbed it and knocked the audience out of their seats.

Screenwriters have the advantage over Schwarzenegger and all the others who work in film. Joe Director has to wait until somebody writes a terrific screenplay before he can go to work again and prove that he is a great "auteur." Josephine Star can't recover from a flop until she discovers a writer who has written a character for her that she can "create."

Screenwriters alone, of all the filmmaking artists, don't have to wait for anybody. It is thus the ultimate irony that all the movieland folk who depend on the screenplay in order to go to work take credit for authorship of it.

The answer to the famous question that a screenwriter posed to director Frank Capra, "Where were you when the pages were blank?" is *unemployed*.

They can reject you, belittle you, steal your authorship, demean you in interviews, but the blunt truth of the matter is that they are all helpless without you. Nobody works in Hollywood until the screenwriter works. Take comfort in knowing that the studio execs, the producers, the directors, the stars, are beggars with their hands out: "Please, screenwriter, give me a screenplay that will make my career."

No matter how shabbily you are treated, when all is said and done, you alone have the power.

There are three reasons for becoming a writer: the first is that you need the money; the second, that you have something to say that you think the world should know; the third is that you can't think what to do with the long evenings.
—Quentin Crisp, *The Naked Civil Servant*

A writer needs three things, experience, observation, and imagination, any two of which, at times any one of which, can supply the lack of the others.
—William Faulkner, from *Writers at Work, 1st Series*

I don't like work—no man does—but I like what is in work—the chance to find yourself. Your own reality—for yourself, not for others—what no other man can ever know.
—Joseph Conrad, *Heart of Darkness*

Dying is Easy, Comedy is Hard

An Interview with

Larry Gelbart

"You've got to tempt failure. It makes success all the sweeter."
—Larry Gelbart

This apocryphal story is legendary in the world of show business: The old actor is lying on his deathbed as several of his young students gather about his frail figure, tears streaming down their faces.

"Don't weep for me, boys and girls," says the veteran actor, "dying is easy. Comedy is hard."

For those of us who have spent our lifetimes writing and producing film and/or television, we know within this little story lies the bedrock truth. Great comedy writers are as rare as the Hope diamond and worth much more.

Suppose you had your choice between owning a diamond mine or being one of the two greatest comedy writers in the history of theater, motion pictures, and television. It's a no-brainer: Choose the latter—diamond mines can bring you a fortune, but a truly great comedy talent can bring you a fortune and a lifetime of laughter.

Hollywood is Mecca to anybody with the talent to put words on paper that will cause people to laugh out loud. Quiet chuckles or big grins won't do it. Only writers with the talent to write "hard" comedy (belly-laugh comedy) need apply. (The blunt truth is that writers of light comedy are a dime a dozen.)

I'm sorry to report that writing funny is not a talent you can learn—you have to be born with it. I'm happy to report that if you have this rare gift, fame and fortune most certainly await you. You can count on one hand the number of truly great comedy writers working in American film, television, and theater.

Towering over the others are two men who write film, TV, and theater: Larry Gelbart and Neil "Doc" Simon. Both of these exceptionally gifted men have written hit Broadway shows, comedy movies that rank among the top ten comedies of all time, television series that set records for both longevity and genuine laughter. Both writers have accumulated credits, awards, and credentials far beyond their fellow specialists in the rarefied field of comedy. And, rarest of all, neither of them need a laugh track.

I am a great admirer of both these comedy geniuses (no doubt they both belong in the genius category). Both writers enjoy the enormous respect, admiration, and even awe of all of us lesser talents. Perhaps most surprising of all, in the ego-driven world of Hollywood, both writers are warmly regarded personally by their fellow writers. In addition to being our greatest living comedy writers, they are not only good people, but humble people.

Arguably the landmark non-star-driven comedy series in the history of television is *M*A*S*H*. It still maintains its enormous popularity several years since the series ceased production simply because it was (and arguably still is) the best-written comedy in the past fifty years. The guiding genius behind this remarkable series (call him auteur, if you insist) was Larry Gelbart. He wrote a majority of the episodes and rewrote scores of others. *M*A*S*H* had Gelbart's imprimatur stamped on every episode. Gelbart's work on *M*A*S*H* alone would put him in anybody's Comedy Writer's Hall of Fame, yet I call your attention to his credits that appear at the end of our brief interview. No comedy writer I'm aware of could surpass his dazzling output.

The most hilarious evening I have ever spent at the theater was one evening on Broadway when my good buddy, the late Rod Serling, and I went to see "A Funny Thing Happened on the Way to the Forum." Years later I bought a laser disc of the movie version, which loses very little in its translation to film. Though my wife and I have watched it several times, our level of enjoyment has not diminished. It's Gelbart at the peak of his form.

I have always wanted to talk to the man who wrote this comedy masterpiece and has given countless hours of laughter to me and my family. Our interview follows. A more charming, less pretentious, and delightful man than Larry Gelbart you are not likely to meet.

[Note: Since our interview, the latest reincarnation of "A Funny Thing Happened on the Way to the Forum," starring Nathan Lane, has opened to rave reviews and SRO business. It's the hottest ticket on Broadway.]

FROUG: When did you decide you were a writer? How young were you when you finally said, This is what I have to do?

GELBART: Well, I started doing it before I thought I *had* to do it. I was very very lucky, I suppose, to become a professional writer while I was still in high school, Fairfax High School in Los Angeles, when I was sixteen.

FROUG: That's pretty early. Were you writing comedy when you started?

GELBART: Yes, on an amateur basis to start with, school stuff. Then I got an opportunity to write some material for Danny Thomas, who was appearing on the Fannie Brice radio show called *Maxwell House Coffee Time*. Thomas had a six- or seven-minute spot all to himself. He played a Walter Mitty-type of character who acted out a fantasy on each show. I seized the opportunity, obviously.

FROUG: Do you think you can teach comedy writing?

GELBART: I don't believe that comedy is an acquired skill. One can appreciate it, and most people do, obviously, but it's very hard to instruct others on how to practice being funny.

FROUG: In twenty-five years of teaching, Larry, I discovered only *three* comedy writers. In twenty-five years!

GELBART: It is a gift, you know. One you don't ask for, and very often one you would like to give back, but it's not something you can learn.

FROUG: Which of the many things you've written means the most to you?

GELBART: "A Funny Thing Happened on the Way to the Forum" was a very special experience for me. That show literally goes back to the origins of stage comedy, based as it was on the twenty-six existing plays that were written by the Roman playwright Plautus some twenty-six hundred years ago. We don't advertise it but, in fact, it is a kind of a scholarly work— a bit of plot from one play, a character from another play, and a great deal of connective tissue. It was more a matter of archaeology. It was really the most challenging thing I've ever done. Having started so young as a writer, I didn't go to college, the work being so consuming. "Forum" was, in a sense, my college experience. I really learned a great deal. I consider myself a graduate of the University of California at Ancient Rome.

"I don't believe that comedy is an acquired skill. One can appreciate it, and most people do, obviously, but it's very hard to instruct others on how to practice being funny."

FROUG: Rod Serling and I went to see "Funny Thing" the first week it opened on Broadway with Zero Mostel, and the two of us just collapsed. I mean we were doubled over, tears of laughter streaming down our cheeks. It's a masterpiece.

GELBART: They're reviving it on Broadway.

FROUG: I heard that and I know financially it's wonderful for you, but I was sorry because how do you improve on a masterpiece?

GELBART: They certainly have my permission to do so. I'm curious to see what the show will mean to audiences a generation and a half down the line.

FROUG: Who can duplicate Zero Mostel?

GELBART: Nobody. A lot of the people involved in the revival, the director and a lot of the cast, will never have seen him in the role, and that is for the better. They won't be intimidated. And no one could be more intimidating than Zero.

You know Hollywood. Nothing succeeds like excess.

FROUG: Which leads me to a question about repeating previous hits. I thought *Oh, God!*, the original you wrote, was hysterically funny. I thought it was another Gelbart masterpiece. But then they proceeded to remake it and remake it and nothing measured up to the original.

GELBART: You know Hollywood. Nothing succeeds like excess. The first time you do something, it has the spark of freshness and invention that comes with covering new ground. The second and third times, its only reason for being is to capitalize on the original's success at the box office. There's no attempt to make it new or fresh or interesting.

FROUG: I think you're right, the excitement is gone. How do you go about writing? Do you outline things before you write them?

GELBART: I've done it both ways. I think eventually I'm happier if I've really thought it out scene by scene because it provides a road map, even if you decide to take a few off-ramps or detours. But I prefer an outline. And very often do it that way.

FROUG: Did you read the *WGA Journal* article last month on the structure gurus?

GELBART: By the time I read an article by a structure guru, he's usually been replaced by another structure guru. So many gurus and so few good movies. Where are all these lessons going?

FROUG: That's a good question.

GELBART: There have never been more film students and there has never been less great work. I recently watched a video of Paddy Chayevsky's *Network*. It was invigorating, astonishing, prescient, and contained none of the elements today's films are filled with—no violence, to our intelligence, that is. The language of the film flies. It soars. Do gurus ever suggest to their students that they must write *beautifully*?

FROUG: What's interesting about Paddy is that he is one of the few screenwriters who insisted words are absolutely vital. He believed in words.

GELBART: That's because he was rooted in theater.

FROUG: Yes he was, and I believe he was the greatest of all the writers to come out of the Golden Age, as they rightly call it, of live television.

"Do gurus ever suggest to their students that they must write beautifully?"

GELBART: No question. Unfortunately, now we have people for whom television was their theater experience, and so the writing gets poorer and poorer . . . we know the rest of this speech . . .

FROUG: Yeah, but what I don't know and I'd love to find out is why, with all of our efforts, puny though they may seem, we can't gain any recognition for writers in either film or television. Why is it that this auteur bullshit has any credence whatsoever? Has anybody ever seen the film a so-called auteur director has done from blank pages?

GELBART: Well, we're more likely to get recognition in television, I believe.

FROUG: Why is that?

GELBART: Writers are given some power in television. In the theater and print, in the beginning there is the word. With movies, in the beginning it was the face. It's what the public really cares most about. Faces on the screen. Words have just always been secondary. Look how many successful silents there were. And then this whole French auteur fraud has really done writers in. Certainly in American films, it has. I don't think we'll ever be allowed to get off the floor.

FROUG: I fear not. For example, I had a student this summer at FSU who read David Peoples' screenplay of *Unforgiven*. And he said, "This screenplay makes me think it's possible that the writer is as important as the director." [Laughter] My God!

GELBART: Hello, Columbus. That's pathetic. It really is.

FROUG: On your "City of Angels," which was a pretty good-sized hit on Broadway, did you have a little more power than you might have on a film?

GELBART: In the theater, it's the writer who calls all the shots. Short of the ultimate power. The producer of a Broadway production has the final say (he can, after all, refuse to raise the curtain). The writer has approval of the director and of the cast. And, of course, there can be no changes whatsoever in the writer's text. It's a Hollywood mogul's worst nightmare come true.

FROUG: I learned from the Guild that not only did you write the *M*A*S*H* pilot but also thirty-six or more episodes.

GELBART: It's closer to ninety-seven. I wrote thirty-six . . .

FROUG: You rewrote the others.

GELBART: You've sat in that chair. You rewrite, you polish, you cut, you spin each script into gold.

FROUG: How in the world could you keep it fresh? How many years did *M*A*S*H* run?

GELBART: Well, *M*A*S*H* ran ten and a half seasons, but I left the series after the first four years. I'd done my best, my worst, and everything in between. So that was it for me. I worked on ninety-seven scripts altogether. That was enough. By about ninety-six scripts.

FROUG: I would think you'd be burned out.

GELBART: Well, I was. I think I could have found ways to continue . . . but so what? So I could turn out to be the person who writes that show better than anyone else in the world? You've got to go on to other things. You've got to tempt failure. It makes success all the sweeter.

FROUG: *Barbarians at the Gate* was a particularly wonderful movie for HBO. Did you have a shot at making that as a feature or did you contract with HBO to make it?

GELBART: It started life as a would-be feature. It was commissioned by Ray Stark, who was going to produce it for Columbia Pictures, but it became increasingly clear to them that the nature of the material was so special they wouldn't risk perhaps forty million dollars on a picture that would have a very limited appeal. The moment the gave up on it, Ray immediately went to HBO and they snapped it up. I think the screenplay reflects a freedom I knew I would have on the big screen as opposed to any sort of self-censorship I might have fallen prey to had I written it directly for television.

FROUG: How about *Mastergate*? That was such a super idea.

GELBART: Originally I was going to write it as a screenplay and then I realized I just didn't want to run the studio/development obstacle course—work for two or three years taking notes from underage executives, playing phone-tag with agents—you know, the minefield. So I wrote it as a play. Bob Brustein at the American Repertory Theater in Cambridge had asked me for a piece, hopefully political in nature, and it seemed a natural. We did it there first, quite successfully, and then we took it to Broadway. We later did the Showtime production, which I don't really think is all that good, but at least I have a record of it. It's a lot like someone taking a terrible picture of one of your children.

FROUG: You wrote about a dozen episodes of the TV series *United States*. You also created *United States*, didn't you?

GELBART: Right. The show, not the country.

FROUG: The good news is, as a writer, there's no chance you will create any country.

GELBART: No, but there are one or two I would dearly love to
rewrite.

FROUG: Which of your TV shows is your favorite? *M*A*S*H*
obviously has to be one that dominates your life.

GELBART: I didn't mean for it to but it has, of course, and a couple
of years on *Caeser's Hour* were really memorable, too.

FROUG: Working with Sid Ceaser must have been a gas.

GELBART: It was. But *M*A*S*H* represents more than just fun.
Except for the usual network and studio idiocies like program
practices and the rating madness, it was like theater for me. I
had a totally free hand. It was an incredible environment in
television to have that freedom and license to speak from your
heart and your mind.

FROUG: It's almost unheard of. You get the feeling that one of
the reasons that show lasted so well, aside from the fact that
it had superb scripts, was because of the rare sense of
camaraderie among the cast. They really seemed to be in
tune with each other.

GELBART: It was a remarkable company of actors. Great soloists
who knew how to fold themselves into an ensemble. There
was occasional friction, but the sparks just seemed to illumi-
nate how gifted they were.

FROUG: Are you into a new TV series now?

GELBART: I haven't got the legs for it anymore, or the hours.

FROUG: What is your next project?

GELBART: I'm ashamed to say how ashamed and appalled I am by
how much I'm doing. I am in a totally manic state. It must be

a race with the embalmer. I seem to have forgotten how to merely do just enough.

FROUG: How many projects can you do at the same time?

GELBART: I'm about to find out. But you know, Bill, from your own experience, that when you're doing a series, you're playing six-dimensional chess all the time. So I'm doing that now, only on different projects. I spend some time working on one, then I shift to another. It's a great system because when you come to a cul-de-sac on project "a," you switch gears and go to "b" or "c." There's some part of your brain, not unlike Microsoft Windows, where there's work going on that you don't know about and when you return to those dead ends, somehow there's an answer to the story you're trying to tell; you've found a door you didn't know was there before. I like mixing it up that way. I can't deny, however, that when you give something your full, full concentration and focus, that work is enriched by your unbroken concentration.

FROUG: But it may also be that you reach a stage in life, as I have, where you're free to do whatever you damn well please. You're no longer in a situation where you take a job because you've got to have some money.

GELBART: Money is just a camouflage for your ego. That's the engine that drives most writers.

"Money is just a camouflage for your ego. That's the engine that drives most writers."

Stronger Than Fiction
by Larry Gelbart

The last thing this country needs is one more victim, but I'm afraid the victims will have to move over and make room for me. Nothing sordid, not a scintilla of titillation. I carry no childhood scars. My welts, all relatively new, have been acquired in my professional, not my personal, life.

I love to write. I could write in the shower if someone ever came out with a laptop on a rope. But what to write about in these times? What is there in my imagination that can compete with the theatrics of reality? Would I dare contrive a story wherein Kobe, Japan, is all but wiped out exactly one year to the day after the quake that devastated Los Angeles? Could I dream up a scenario that depicted the ongoing destruction of the jungles of Brazil? One that showed people using the Amazon forest for kindling? Just to make room for cattle to graze? Torching and decimating one of the wonders of the planet so that we can have our uninterrupted supply of Big Macs? Could I conceive a religious cult that accumulates enough toxic material to kill a hundred million people, after getting high on their leader's bath water? Can I compete with that kind of drama—drama that so finely mixes tragedy and absurdity?

One of the first to comment on the phenomenon, the near-impossibility of any Muse to compete with the news, was the sportswriter Red Smith. In 1951, in one of the most memorable sports moments of all time, the then-New York Giants and the also-then-Brooklyn Dodgers, after a tense, nail-biting season, were slugging it out in the final playoff game that would determine the winner of the National League pennant. In the bottom of the ninth inning, Bobby Thompson clinched the pennant for the Giants by hitting the improbable, miraculous home run that inspired Red Smith to write: "The art of fiction is dead. Reality has strangled invention. Only the utterly impossible, the inexpressibly fantastic, can ever be plausible again."

Fast-forward forty years. I'm commissioned to update a 1937 movie classic, *Nothing Sacred*, the story of a small-town girl who lies about having a terminal illness and becomes a national celebrity when a big-town newspaper publicizes her plight. During the period on which I worked on the script, real-life events packed with unimaginable drama began to unfold at a remarkable rate, events that demonstrated that the mixture of modern-day technology with the public's insatiable appetite for gossip and scandal made notoriety possible in the blink of the television camera's eye.

It became increasingly clear that there was no way I could update the script successfully. Lying about your health is small change in today's hype-happy society. Commit a murder, or two or three or four. Rape somebody. Beat someone. Or be beaten. Be part of any ugliness that offends people so much that they can't get enough of it, and you, too, can be a star. You, too, can have your fifteen minutes of infamy.

Consider just some of the incidents that unfolded while I was trying to write my script: the beating of Rodney King, repeated on television so often it began to take on the aspects of a test pattern. That drill in sadism triggered the Rodney King trial, and—Hollywood being Hollywood—the sequel to the Rodney King trial, with a catastrophic riot serving as an intermission.

That riot gave us the Reginald Denny beating, complete with his own tape and his own trial, during which he hugged the mothers of the men who shattered his skull into so many Scrabble pieces.

In that same period, we were also treated to the spectacle of Judge Clarence Thomas's Supreme Court confirmation hearings, with Prof. Anita Hill giving Coca-Cola millions of dollars of free publicity by going public about matters pubic.

Then there were the Jimmy Swaggart scandals, followed by the Jim and Tammy Bakker follies. For a while there, all we could hear was the sound of commandments breaking and smashing all around us.

In the sporting world, Mike Tyson went to jail for hitting below the belt. In his hotel room.

Meanwhile, in the civilized world, we learned of the unspeakable acts of Jeffrey Dahmer and John Wayne Gacy. The latter, who was convicted of murdering more than thirty young men, established an 800 number from his cell on Death Row for those who wanted to hear his taped plea of innocence, becoming the nation's first serial killer for serial callers.

The country also had its necessary, periodic Kennedy fix, becoming mesmerized by the Willie Smith rape trial, during which we learned that Master Smith had a penchant for young women with blue dots for faces.

Then there were the revelations about Magic Johnson, revelations that ended an awful lot of hoop dreams, including his own.

There were the charges against Michael Jackson, and those against the brothers Menendez, who, having put their parents in their boxes, ended up on our own.

We had the John and Lorena Bobbitt story, which taught us the infinite possibilities of recycling.

And the poignant saga of Joey Buttafuoco and Amy Fisher—probably the first couple in the history of heat to make love under a car.

We had the demonic David Koresh and the Branch Dividian hold-out and, finally, flameout.

We had the then-just-beginning, but probably never-ending, Whitewater affair.

We were witnesses to Tonya Harding's effort to break Nancy Kerrigan's spirit, starting with her kneecaps.

And, of course, there was the start of the O.J. Simpson trial, which all of us have now been sentenced to watch for life.

All this, in addition to the nonstop lineup of misfits, weirdos and psychopaths who spill their guts and their secrets, daily and nightly, on Oprah, or Geraldo, or Donahue, or Montel, or Ricki, or Maury, or Jerry, or Jenny, or Leeza, or any of the other sleazeathons that tell us far more than any one of us ever wanted to know about the freaks next door: the flashers and the bashers, the batterers and the batterees, the adulterous adolescent bridegrooms, their teenage mates in maternity grunge, the drag queens and the porn kings, the pimps and the simps, the topless, the mindless, the cuckolds, the Kluxers, the neo-Nazis—the Niagra of nauseating nutsies we allow on our living room screens that we wouldn't let get past our front doors.

Add to that programs like *A Current Affair* and *Hard Copy* and *Inside Edition* and publications that range from the *National Enquirer* to far more traditional, establishment newspapers steadily lowering their real or imagined standards by dishing out ever more dirt on ever more people, even those willing to dish it out about themselves. To say nothing of the television networks, which have, in their pursuit of ratings and revenue, dropped nearly all pretense of quality reporting and now bring us such timely events as ABC's devoting a full hour to the Charles Manson story, twenty-five years after his grotesque acts, acts committed while we still had a thimbleful of shock left in us.

With all of the promises of an information superhighway, all we get are only more and more keyholes to peek in. Surely there ought to be a way the public could be weaned away, given some relief from all this. The short-term guilty pleasure we get from wallowing in prurience and sensationalism has the harmful, long-term effect of desensitizing us, making us immune to outrage, so heavy is the air with outrageous acts. A good start might be for the media to cut down on the number of minutes or inches of space they devote to the seamier events of the day. Perhaps that kind of reportage could be confined to cable, to a kind of human misery channel. Ideally, we ourselves might somehow try to curb our appetite for human tragedy and foolishness. Maybe if someone discovered that bad news is fattening? Or that chaos causes cholesterol?

I'm not saying the world would be a better place if we tried a new approach. This world stubbornly, doggedly refuses to be a better place. For proof, see Bosnia or Chechnya. See Somalia. See Palestine or Rwanda. Or just see Washington, DC—especially if you enjoy watching three-piece suits mud wrestling. But I do know that by watching and reading as much mind- and soul-numbing material as we're exposed to, we only validate the cynical attitude of the providers of that material.

Perhaps all things being cyclical, this fixation with those among us who would not only kill for our attention but actually do kill for our attention will one day diminish. And on that heavenly day, those of us who have to write because it's the one way we prove to ourselves that we're still alive, will be able to put our imaginations back into gear. Once again, we'll be able to engage your hearts and some brighter corners of your curiosity. We might even ask you to join us and indulge yourself in a little hope.

(© Larry Gelbart, reprinted courtesy of the author)

CREDITS

Radio:

Danny Thomas (*Maxwell House Coffee Time*)

Duffy's Tavern

The Eddie Cantor Show

The Jack Carson Show

The Joan Davis Show

The Bob Hope Show

The Jack Paar Show

Command Performance (Armed Forces Radio Service)

Television:

The Bob Hope Show

The Red Buttons Show

Honestly, Celeste! (The Celeste Holm Show)

The Patrice Munsel Show

The Pat Boone Show

Caesar's Hour

The Art Carney Specials

The Danny Kaye Show (developed and consulted—first season)

The Marty Feldman Comedy Machine (Writer/Producer)

M★A★S★H (developed for TV, principal writer, sometime
   director and co-producer, first four seasons)
   (Emmy Award, with Co-Producer Gene Reynolds)

United States (created)

AfterMASH (developed)

*1985 Academy of Motion Picture Arts and Sciences Award
   Show* (Writer/Co-Producer)

1986 Academy of Motion Picture Arts and Sciences Award
    Show (Writer)
Mastergate

Motion Pictures:
  Notorious Landlady, Columbia, 1962
  The Thrill of it All, Universal, 1963
  The Wrong Box, Columbia, 1966 (also Associate Producer)
  Oh, God!, Warner Bros., 1978
    (Oscar nomination)
  Movie Movie, Warner Bros., 1978
  Neighbors, Columbia, 1981
  Tootsie, Columbia, 1982
    (Oscar nomination)
  Blame It on Rio, 20th Century-Fox, 1984 (also Executive
    Producer)
  Barbarians at the Gate, HBO, 1993
    (Emmy Award, Outstanding Made-for-Television Movie)

Theater:
  My L.A.
  The Conquering Hero
  A Funny Thing Happened on the Way to the Forum
    (Tony Award)
  Jump
  Sly Fox
  Mastergate
  City of Angels
    (Tony Awards, Best Book and Best Musical)
  Power Failure

Writers Guild of America Awards:

Oh, God!

Movie Movie

Tootsie

M*A*S*H (three episodes)

Barbarians at the Gate

Additional Awards Include:

Humanitas Award, *M*A*S*H*

Peabody Award, *M*A*S*H* and *The Danny Kaye Show*

Christopher Award, *Movie Movie*

Los Angeles Film Critics' Award, Best Screenplay, *Tootsie*

New York Film Critics' Award, Best Screenplay, *Tootsie*

National Society of Film Critics Award, Best Screenplay, *Tootsie*

Outer Critics Circle Award, Outstanding Broadway Musical,
   City of Angels

New York Drama Critics Circle, Best New Musical, *City of Angels*

London Critics' Drama Award, Best New Musical, *City of Angels*

Golden Globe Award, Miniseries of Telefilm, *Barbarians at the Gate*

A Writer for all Seasons and all Reasons

An Interview with

Stuart Kaminsky

"As you know, the number of new screenwriters who actually have the determination to keep going, to be able to take the constant shock of rejection in the industry, is small. The point I want to make is if you don't think you have much of a chance, if you think the odds are too great, you're right. When I worked for Don Siegel at Universal, for example, there were so many scripts coming in every week that I took home ten screenplays every night, and so did everybody else. So why should a writer even try? Why do this? If you can't answer that question for yourself, I'll not answer it for you. I'll answer it for me. I have one life to live, and there are a certain number of films that are going to be made. I want to be one who makes some of those. So, yeah, I'm going to buck the odds because that's what I want to do. I gotta do it."

—Stuart Kaminsky

Stuart Kaminsky is a writer's writer and a teacher's teacher, a top-selling novelist, biographer, film scholar, screenwriter, short-story writer, film essayist, and founder and former Director of the Florida State University Conservatory of Motion Pictures, Television, and the Recording Arts, as well as professor of screenwriting. His mystery novels have sold over a million copies worldwide and are published in many foreign-language editions.

Our discussions on screenwriting have been ongoing since my move to Sarasota three years ago, and have led to a close friendship, in part, because we both have strong opinions that often generate lively debate.

Kaminsky, who gives new meaning and depth to the word prolific, has a great deal to say that is both original and important to the beginning screenwriter, which is why he was the first writer I asked to be in this book.

What you have here is a world-class, master storyteller.

FROUG: You began your career as a film teacher at North-
        western, didn't you?

KAMINSKY: I began as a little kid in Chicago cutting school to go
        see movies. I had a great love of film. I cut summer camp
        almost every day to go to movies, and there were only two
        movie theaters reasonably close and that I could afford. One
        was in a Russian movie theater, which only showed Russian

movies. They were open half an hour earlier than the other one; I saw the Russian classics.

FROUG: That was your beginning?

KAMINSKY: I began writing when I was very young. Between the ages of eleven and fourteen, I started to write seriously, never thinking that I was going to make a career of it. It was just something I did. I didn't know what I was going to do for a living, maybe become a botanist or something. I wrote short stories; I wrote poetry. Except for a few poems in English classes, I never showed them to anybody. I wrote one of my favorite stories when I was about fourteen, and I decided to submit it to two friends of mine, twins, who were running a mimeographed literary magazine. It was a short story called "Christ Lives in a Chicago Hotel." They rejected it. [Laughter] I had my first rejection from my best friends, which discouraged me mightily. It discouraged me to go on and on, continuing to write with little success—very, very little.

FROUG: Writing short stories?

KAMINSKY: I did quite a few short stories. Once in a while, I had something published: *The New Mexico Quarterly* published a story of mine; *The Man From U.N.C.L.E.* magazine did five of my stories. The maximum I was getting was thirty-five to fifty dollars a story. I had a short play produced off Broadway but it didn't do anything.

FROUG: How did you get to Northwestern?

KAMINSKY: First, I did my undergraduate work in Journalism at the University of Illinois. I did not do particularly well. I basically spent a lot of time staying home reading and not

"Between the ages of eleven and fourteen, I started to write seriously, never thinking that I was going to make a career of it. It was just something I did."

getting up in the morning, so I barely squeaked by. I also spent an enormous amount of time at the campus newspaper. I was a reporter, and I loved it. I would stay up all night, volunteering to write. I worked for a couple for newspapers and United Press. I went in the Army, where I found out there was a program for getting out of the Army two months early if you were in a graduate program. So I went back to Champaign/Urbana and did graduate work at the University of Illinois. Then I went on to write for some dull publications, all the time writing novels—writing one, two, three, four, five, six novels.

FROUG: Mystery novels or all kinds of novels?

KAMINSKY: All kinds of novels. Mostly they were pretentious art novels.

FROUG: But nobody was buying?

KAMINSKY: Nobody was terribly interested. I got into university public relations at the University of Illinois, then at the University of Michigan, then at the University of Chicago. I began to move up the administrative ranks at the University of Chicago until one day I decided that, even though I was well paid, I was on the lower end of the academic totem pole. So I decided to go back to school, get a Ph.D., and do what these guys were doing, because it looked awfully easy. [Laughter] I applied for the Ph.D. program in Journalism at Northwestern. When I got there, they accepted me, and then they eliminated the doctorate program in Journalism. So I switched my major to film. I didn't even know you could teach film. You watch films all day? And talk about 'em? This is crazy. [Laughter] It was wonderful. I got my Ph.D. faster than anybody. It's a Ph.D. in speech. In parenthesis, it says it's film and television. I also had a strong minor emphasis in theater.

FROUG: When I mentioned your name to my former student Laury Dworet, he told me that the best book about film genre was written by Stuart Kaminsky. How did that come about?

KAMINSKY: It was something that hit me early on in graduate school. That was during the height of the auteur theory—a popular theory that films are primarily the work of the director—but I thought, Wait, that's not why I go to see movies. I go to see movies by categories: It's a hell of an adventure movie. It's a gangster movie, it's a Western, it's a horror movie, whatever they're selling. I'm not saying, "Oh, it's directed by Roland B. Lee so I'd better go see it." But I couldn't find anything that had been written on film genres, except for something by a couple of French guys, in French. So I decided to start writing papers about that. One of the first papers I did was on film genre, which the professor didn't like. He said that it didn't have enough feeling, enough heart. Anyway, I kept writing papers about the history of movie genres. And when I got my degree, I had already taught a couple of graduate classes, so the head of the department offered me a teaching job. I took the job immediately, and I was there for seventeen years. I wound up as head of the department.

FROUG: You must have a part of you that loves teaching?

KAMINSKY: Oh, I absolutely love teaching.

FROUG: While you were teaching, how many books did you turn out?

KAMINSKY: If we don't count the five that were not published, over thirty, fiction and non-fiction. By this point I also had twenty-five or thirty short stories published.

FROUG: Have you added to that?

KAMINSKY: I've added to that. I think I'm getting close to forty novels. I think I'm approaching fifty books.

FROUG: And almost all of them are still in print, aren't they?

KAMINSKY: Yes. All of my novels, with one exception, are still in print.

FROUG: About how many copies of your novels have been sold to date?

KAMINSKY: Well over a million, worldwide.

FROUG: Do you feel that writing novels is a good way for film students to get into screenwriting?

KAMINSKY: It's a round-about way to writing movies. I think that everybody makes their own way. Whatever works for you won't necessarily work for somebody else. For me, it was through writing the novels.

FROUG: You also wrote a couple films during this period. You wrote screenplays for *A Woman in the Wind* and *Enemy Territory*.

KAMINSKY: Yes. Even though I was a film teacher, my screenwriting clearly came from being a novelist.

FROUG: Because people read your novels and said, "Gee, I'd like to see that guy write a screenplay"?

KAMINSKY: I wrote my first screenplay, *Enemy Territory*, on spec. I sent it to my agent, who sent it to another agent, who liked it and sold it very quickly. Then, a bit later, I was contacted by Sergio Leone. I'd written two published articles about him, but he had no idea about that. He'd read my novels in Italian, in Italy, where they're very, very popular. His nephew read my novels, his wife read my novels, his daughter read my novels, and he was looking for an American writer who could write gangster dialogue for *Once Upon a Time in America*. I was taking a nap one afternoon when my young son says, "There's someone on the phone, Dad." I said, "Who is it." And he says, "It's Sergio Leone." I thought it was one of my friends playing a joke. I said, "I don't know who it is, but get a number, I'll call them back." But my son says, "Dad, the man says he really has to talk to you now." So I got on the phone and the guy calling couldn't speak English, so another guy, one of his assistants, said, "Sergio Leone wants to ask you some questions." And I hear this voice in the background asking questions in Italian. I got a little wary.

FROUG: Had you begun to believe him yet?

KAMINSKY: No, I still didn't know if it was a joke or not. He said, "The important thing is where you are from." I said, "Chicago." Sergio said, "Wonderful, wonderful, wonderful!" He said, "This is an important question. Are you Jewish?" Now my back is up; I'm getting a little more wary. What difference does it make? I said, "Yes," and there's this outcry, "Wonderful! Wonderful! Can you be in New York City at the Plaza Hotel tomorrow?" [Laughter] I got to the Plaza Hotel and found out that he had interviewed eighteen other writers. He interviewed me, and I got along extremely well with him.

FROUG: Even though he spoke no English?

KAMINSKY: He spoke no English. We got along very well with interpreters. Eventually, he hired me to write the dialogue. He had no dialogue, just a story. You know how European scripts look: The dialogue is on one side of the page and on the other side is the action. He had a long, long synopsis—a treatment of 124 pages, which he and three other writers had been working on for eight years. He said, "Your job is to write what they say. You do all the characters, then we'll come back and talk about them. If you get any ideas other than dialogue, you give 'em to me and we'll kick 'em around with everybody else."

I was on the film for nine months. I spent four months in Italy while they were building the sets. I spent a total of a month and a half in Los Angeles. I worked with Robert DeNiro for one week and I worked with other writers for a while. I did my work with the other Italian writers in Rome and with other Leone writers in New York City. I personally wrote five drafts of the film. The first draft was 350 pages. And he wasn't bothered at all.

FROUG: He didn't mind a three- or four-hour film?

KAMINSKY: He didn't care. He looked at it and he made me sit there while he read it. Actually, it was translated for him and explained to him. It was a delight because here's this little rotund Italian man reading it and laughing. He was laughing and laughing with tears in his eyes. Then he said, "This is very funny. I don't want a funny movie." There is nothing left from that first draft of mine in the final film.

FROUG: Had you attempted to be funny?

KAMINSKY: I thought that was why I was hired—to make a funny movie. In his other movies, he had things that were very humorous. *The Good, the Bad, and the Ugly* is a funny movie. I thought that's what he wanted. Apparently not. So we kept doing drafts and getting more and more serious. As I said, I worked on it for nine months.

FROUG: Were you well-paid?

KAMINSKY: Yes. And it was fun. I worked most of the time on my own in a hotel in Rome.

FROUG: How did you like the movie when it came out?

KAMINSKY: Leone's final cut was over three hours in length. The Ladd Company decided to cut it down to two hours. When they finished butchering it, it was a two-hour disaster. Critics who have seen the original three-hour version, which was released later, have given it four stars and called it a masterpiece.

FROUG: During this period, you were still teaching film?

KAMINSKY: Yeah, but I was on sabbatical leave. I was going to write the official biography of Patricia Neal. I had a contract. It was all set. I worked with her, got along reasonably well with her, and wrote several samples chapters. When I sent the chapters to her, it fell through because of her husband, Roald Dahl. I got a letter back from him saying that this book is not going to be done because it's about her and Gary Cooper. I didn't put anything in there that she hadn't given me. It was exactly what she'd given me. The contract was canceled. Then, coincidentally, I got this phone call from Sergio Leone. A film job is much better than writing a biography.

FROUG: Did you have an agent handling all this?

KAMINSKY: My book agent is Dominick Abel. All of my books have been sold through Dominick. I have a literary agent who offers sub rights, so I've got a bunch of sub-rights sales. I have a film agent in Los Angeles who handles certain book properties of mine. I have another film agent in New York who handles the Toby Peters series. And I have another agent who handles original film works of mine.

FROUG: What are sub rights? Is that the same thing that the Writers Guild defines as ancillary rights?

KAMINSKY: It's similar. For example, I've got agents in Europe and Asia for foreign languages, but they all work through my primary agent in New York.

FROUG: You once mentioned to me that you have a contract to turn out a book a year for each of three different publishers.

KAMINSKY: Yes, but I have no contract at all with my agent. I have never had a contract with him, other than a handshake. Dominick was an editor at a publishing company, Regnery. I submitted a book proposal to them and he called me in and said, "We don't want the book, but I like the way you write. I'm going to become an agent and I'll take you on if you're interested." Dominick's been my agent ever since.

FROUG: So this prolific writing career is going on at the same time you're teaching film?

KAMINSKY: I wasn't writing as many.

FROUG: And somewhere in the in-between minutes, you were also writing biographies of movie stars?

KAMINSKY: I had a contract to write a biography of Charlton Heston. We got along very well, and we worked on it for a year. Then he decided that he wanted to write his own story, so he bought out the contract. My feeling about the biographies I've written, mostly of film people, is that it's their life. They have a right to decide what they want in it. I wrote the first book on Clint Eastwood. When I sent it to the publisher, the publisher asked, "Where's the sex?" And I said that there's not going to be any, that's not what the book is about. It's about his career as an actor and a director. They gave me some trouble, and the person who went to bat for me was Leonard Maltin, my editor.

FROUG: You spent time with Eastwood?

KAMINSKY: Sure. I was the first one to interview him as a director. I went to the prescreening of his first film, *Play Misty for Me*. He also directed a couple of short films and several scenes in *Dirty Harry*. I interviewed him about directing those scenes and I interviewed him generally about his career.

FROUG: Did you foresee this megastar in the making?

KAMINSKY: He was already a megastar, although the industry had ridiculed him. I don't know if you remember back in the '70s, he was sort of like a joke—you know, the action hero who can't act. Then *Life* magazine came out while *Dirty Harry* was being edited, saying that, believe it or not, the most popular actor in the world is Clint Eastwood. I was working on the book at the time.

FROUG: You also did a book about Don Siegel, didn't you?

KAMINSKY: My first published book was *Don Siegel, Director.* I worked for him, and he was extremely nice to me. I clearly consider him my mentor. I wanted to do my dissertation on a director—this was when the auteur theory was really big. I wanted to pick out one of the American directors who had already been identified by the Europeans as an auteur and follow his career through a film or two, see what decisions he really made, and see if he bore out the auteur theory. I didn't know how the industry worked at that point.

Don was extremely kind to me. He hired me, gave me an office right next to his, and basically made me his assistant. He made himself available at all times. He'd include me at all meetings and let me look through all the files. I wrote the dissertation about how he worked on each film, how the process worked, who made the decisions when the scripts were changed, how decisions were made while shooting, the relationships of producers, actors, writers, everything.

FROUG: And you found what?

KAMINSKY: When I turned in my dissertation at Northwestern, they thought it was fine, but they said it was missing something: the analysis of the director as creator.

FROUG: As auteur?

KAMINSKY: Basically, yes, auteur. I told the committee that I believe there are directors who are outstanding, well-educated, brilliant, and Don's one of them, but this whole idea of calling them auteurs is ridiculous. They said, "Well, you've got to do something." So I wrote this last part of the dissertation.

I took all the Siegel films, and I made up this thing about anti-heroes being the continuing link in his films, somehow proving he was a genuine auteur. I made connections.

FROUG: Between the films?

KAMINSKY: You can give ten literary works, ten films at random to any capable professor at that level and say, "Play the game. Connect the dots."

FROUG: It's like the screenwriting theorists—the so-called story-structure gurus—who invent theories that make no sense whatsoever and then they prove that their theories are correct by using their own arcane inventions as proof. They seem to believe screenwriting is all a matter of mathematical equations.

KAMINSKY: They love it. They come up with it and everything fits.

FROUG: Did Siegel read your dissertation?

KAMINSKY: Oh, yeah. It was published without that last section, which I didn't want in it, by Curtis Books. Don read it and he liked it. He had a couple of suggestions, but he was never going to censor me. He said it was my book and all he would do is point out any factual errors. I could do with it what I would.

FROUG: He took to heart your section on him as auteur.

KAMINSKY: He certainly did, but he'd already been recognized by the French and some of the British.

FROUG: Don took it to heart so much that one night when we were playing bridge, we got into a friendly argument over the auteur theory, which he espoused and I think is nonsense, and he insisted that I bring my UCLA students out to his office at Universal to prove to them that he was the auteur of his newest movie, *Charlie Verrick*. He gave us every piece of material written on *Charlie Verrick* from its inception. First we discovered he had discarded Howard Rodman's screenplay and also had a Peter Bogdanovich script, which he had Dean Riesner rewrite. The memos back and forth between Don and the writers were a mess. We read everything, and then, when the picture was finished, Don asked the students out to Universal to see the movie and meet with him for an interview about the film. All the students' papers said about the same thing: Don Siegel is not an auteur. According to the students, he fucked up every *Charlie Verrick* script. I was totally surprised. I never showed the papers to Don. They all hated the film and blamed Siegel.

KAMINSKY: I like *Charlie Verrick*.

FROUG: We disagree, but Siegel was certainly Eastwood's mentor.

KAMINSKY: Oh, absolutely. Clint Eastwood will tell you that. He idolized Don. When Eastwood made his first film, he purposely set up the shooting schedule so that Don would act in the first scene, making Eastwood more comfortable directing it. Don's the bartender in *Play Misty for Me*. They shot that scene first so Siegel could make suggestions about how to shoot it.

FROUG: Let's get back to Kaminsky. What are you finding out about the screenwriting talent of your students? Are you seeing hope for these kids?

KAMINSKY: Yeah, but there's such a small number that really have the talent and the drive. At Northwestern, I started a four-semester honors program that is similar to what you did at UCLA. It was a program in creative writing for the media to which students from various departments in the School of Speech would apply—they'd send in scripts. Somewhat to my surprise and delight for the students, I wound up turning out television writers.

FROUG: My UCLA students were only interested in writing feature films; why were yours going toward TV writing?

KAMINSKY: Because so many Northwestern alums were successful in the television business, they would hire these kids for internships, and the kids were good.

FROUG: They were moving to Hollywood?

KAMINSKY: Yes. They would get internships from Garry Marshall and Bob Banner, and then they'd write a script for whatever it happened to be—*Laverne & Shirley*, *The Odd Couple*. They got their careers started that way.

FROUG: Did you find real comedy writing talent?

KAMINSKY: Yeah, I found some who turned out to be very, very good. As you know, the number who will actually have the determination to keep going, to take the constant shock of rejection, is small. Before we proceed, the point I want to make is if you think you don't have much of a chance, if you think the odds are too great, you're right. When I worked for Don Siegel at Universal, for example, there were so many scripts coming in every week that I took home ten screen-plays every night, and so did everybody else. So why should a

"I've been doing this professionally for well over twenty years, and my normal day is spent writing and thinking about what I'm writing."

writer even try? Why do this? If you can't answer that question for yourself, I'll not answer it for you. I'll answer it for me. I have one life to live, and there are a certain number of films that are going to be made. I want to be one who makes some of those. So, yeah, I'm going to buck the odds because that's what I want to do. I gotta do it.

FROUG: Well, that's what you did as a novelist. You wrote six novels that nobody bought, but you kept writing nonetheless.

KAMINSKY: Writing and rewriting and rewriting and rewriting.

FROUG: You are in your heart and soul and guts a writer. Nothing can change that, can it?

KAMINSKY: Nothing. I've been doing this professionally for well over twenty years, and my normal day is spent writing and thinking about what I'm writing.

FROUG: How many hours do you actually put in at your keyboard?

KAMINSKY: Now that I'm writing full-time, I shoot for about three to four hours every morning. I'd like to do that Monday through Sunday, but it doesn't always work out that way.

FROUG: How many pages of a novel will you turn out in an average day?

KAMINSKY: I will turn out a minimum of ten to twelve pages. I won't miss a deadline. If I'm really under the gun, twenty pages is not unusual. I've turned out as many as twenty-seven pages in a day, but not a three-hour day.

FROUG: Do you outline your books?

KAMINSKY: I outline. The few times I didn't, when I just thought I wanted to see what happens, it took me longer to write the book.

FROUG: When you write a screenplay, do you outline your scenes?

KAMINSKY: Yes. I do a treatment for myself. When I first started, I used to do scene breakdowns for the treatment, but not anymore.

FROUG: You're known to be a human film encyclopedia.

KAMINSKY: We could play this game now: You name some obscure film for me and I will give you lightning-fast facts about it.

FROUG: I've heard you do it many times. You have total recall of every movie you've ever seen. You recall the name of everybody involved in the production. You are a true movie nut.

KAMINSKY: I read every film book that came out. This was a long time before film books were popular. The first book I actually fell in love with was Paul Rotha's *The Film Till Now*. I'd go to the library and read it over and over again. I would study credits, and I had all kinds of favorites. I had nobody to talk to about this stuff, either. I was on my own. But I loved film from the time I was eight or nine years old. I would have been happy going to films three times a day.

FROUG: But you didn't have a desire to move to Hollywood?

KAMINSKY: Never. Although I always seem to find some reason to be out there for a few months a year: I spent summers working for Don Siegel. When I worked on the Charlton Heston book, I spent a couple of summers out there. And I worked for Cornel Wilde's company for a while, doing treatments for books that he purchased.

"I think that someone who can make characters come alive can be taught stories and can work with people who can tell stories. But if you can't make your characters come to life, if you can't write dialogue, if you don't care about these people, then I don't care how big your story is."

FROUG: What do you look for in a student's screenplay that makes you feel that this student has a chance of making it?

KAMINSKY: It differs with different people. I look for dialogue that reveals character. I think that someone who can make characters come alive can be taught stories and can work with people who can tell stories. But if you can't make your characters come to life, if you can't write dialogue, if you don't care about these people, then I don't care how big your story is.

FROUG: I couldn't agree with you more.

KAMINSKY: Obviously you need a story, but in order of importance: dialogue and character, which are hard to separate, and then the story. People make interesting movies, fascinating movies with just two characters sitting in a room talking. What those characters are saying is interesting enough.

FROUG: *My Dinner with Andre*, for example?

KAMINSKY: Yes, or *Clerks*. It doesn't happen that often, but it happens. When I teach screenwriting classes, I tell my students that if you ever get to the point when you say to yourself, "What will my character say next?" you're in big trouble, because those characters aren't alive to you. If they're alive, they say whatever they're going to say and fill out your scene the way you've outlined it. They take care of themselves. They speak for themselves. Some students can do that. A big problem for beginning writers is inflexibility. Inflexibility among the young.

FROUG: That happens a lot, doesn't it?

KAMINSKY: Yes. You often get people who have a good basic idea, fairly good characters, and reasonably good dialogue, but don't want to do the work to improve it because they're convinced that what they've got is as good as it comes. Or they'll stick with their first draft of the script, thinking, This is my script, I've got to go out and sell it. I know people who've spent ten years trying to sell the same damn script—their first script—and that's not the way it works. You just keep going and going and going. You learn by doing it.

I just kept doing it. I'm not completely self-taught, but pretty close to it. I never took a screenwriting course. At the University of Illinois, I took a short-story writing course, to which I owe a great deal. I had written a story about me and my grandfather—my grandfather sitting there, an old man, me a thirteen-year-old kid who wants to go out and play baseball. Just two people in a room talking. This old man wants to prepare me for my Bar Mitzvah and is very bad at communicating; he doesn't speak English. He probably really loves me, but can't really feel it, and I, as a character, feel guilty, wanting to get it all over with. I didn't know whether I'd written a story or not, but the teacher calls me to his office and says that this is one of the best things he has ever read. "You're very, very good. You should consider a career as a writer." I thought, my God, I've been doing this since I was fourteen years old and nobody has ever told me that. That really gave me the encouragement to go on.

FROUG: It started you on your career?

KAMINSKY: That gave me the confidence. This person who I respected, and who was very respected, thought that I was a writer.

[307]

FROUG: You wrote that story out of your own feelings, didn't you?

KAMINSKY: Out of my own experience: what it felt like to be sitting in that room and what I thought my grandfather might be feeling. I just described it. I didn't worry about symbolism, which was the big thing of the time, I didn't worry about anything except telling this little story about two generations—about how I felt about the inability of these two generations to communicate. That's all. I didn't even really think about the generations, I just thought about me and my grandfather sitting at that dining room table.

FROUG: What you had, without even realizing it, was a tremendous theme.

KAMINSKY: Yeah, I didn't realize it at all.

FROUG: Do you urge your students to have a theme going in?

KAMINSKY: No, quite the opposite. I want to know the story and I want to know something about the characters. I don't want any lessons, I don't want anybody telling me how I should think about the world. I want a story where something happens with good dialogue and people. You don't have to sit down and ask, "What's the theme?" It will be there because it's inside of you, because of who you are. I never ever sat down to write a book or a script for which I consciously had a theme in mind. But at the same time, after I've read the reviews and heard the feedback, they'll always come back to me and say the basic theme here is . . . And I agree with them.

FROUG: But you're unaware of it?

"You don't have to sit down and ask, 'What's the theme?' It will be there because it's inside of you, because of who you are."

KAMINSKY: I'm completely unaware of it until they bring it out. Then I look at them and say, "That's the truth, yep."

FROUG: Do you feel that a good screenplay, or a good book, whether it's preplanned or not, has to have a good theme?

KAMINSKY: It has to, but then again, I don't believe the theme comes before the story. I think the whole thing comes, and you are part of it. You pick the subject that will explore a particular theme, but you do not censor that subject. I feel that if you get a racist bigot up there and he's a great character who starts saying things and overwhelming your central figure because what he's saying is so much more powerful, let 'em do it. Let 'em do it because that's in you, and if you let it come out, it's going to be much more powerful. Occasionally, some of my readers criticize something I write as being anti-feminist or not sensitive enough to older people, or X-Y-Z. My answer has always been that I just don't care. This is what the characters say, this is who they are, this is what I write, and I'm not going to stop it. If you don't like them, don't read my books. That's what I want the students to do. To let that happen. It's not a mechanical process. I think there are basics that you need to know going into writing a screenplay: You really do need to know simple things, like how many pages is this? What ratio do you want between dialogue, action, and description? If you've got a three-act structure, what is it? Are there certain things you can do? There are a variety ways of teaching these things, all of them coming out of experience. The way I teach it is different from the way you teach it.

FROUG: Every teacher teaches it differently.

KAMINSKY: Sure, it comes out of our own experiences, and if it works for that student, fine. I think that the technique, the craft, can be taught. If you can teach the craft, you can get people to be very successful writers. It's possible to succeed just by mastering craft.

FROUG: Do you think theme and attitude are synonymous? Does the writer's attitude toward a given story make the theme?

KAMINSKY: Sure, unconsciously. I'll give you an example from the book I'm writing right now. I know from the treatment that this book is going to be about bigotry and racism because I know what is going to happen. It's going to be about gangs in Chicago and the desecration of the synagogue and various other things. What I'm going to say about it, I don't know. I do know that when it's finished, it will reflect what I believe about this issue. Do I know consciously what's going to happen there? No, I don't know.

FROUG: Is it reasonable to assume that it's not going to be a book that's pro-racist?

KAMINSKY: It's reasonable to assume that it will not, but it is not reasonable to assume that I will not have racist characters who are interesting, intelligent, capable, maybe even likable.

FROUG: Because you want multidimensional characters?

KAMINSKY: I think too many scripts go the other way. Someone says they're gonna write a book, a novel, or a screenplay about racism, and you know every racist is going to be bad. If you know your story, it will take you to interesting and complex characters and situations, and sometimes they will surprise you. That's the joy of writing.

"If you know your story, it will take you to interesting and complex characters and situations, and sometimes they will surprise you."

CREDITS

Non-Fiction Books:

Writing for Television, 1988

American Television Genres, 1984

Basic Filmmaking, 1981 (with Dana Hodgdon)

Coop: The Life and Legend of Gary Cooper, 1980

John Houston: Maker of Magic, 1978

Ingmar Bergman: Essays in Criticism, 1975 (edited with
Joseph H. Hill)

American Film Genres, 1974

Clint Eastwood, 1974

Don Siegel: Director, 1973

Novels:

Nineteen mysteries in the Toby Peters series (latest is *Dancing
in the Dark*, 1995)

Ten mysteries in the Porfiry Rostnikov series (latest is *Blood
and Rubles,* 1995)

Four in the Abraham Lieberman series (latest is *Lieberman's
Law*, 1996)

Opening Shots, 1991 (short-story collection)

Exercise in Terror, 1985

When the Dark Man Calls, 1983

Films:

When the Dark Man Calls, 1995 (story, based on Kaminsky's
novel of the same name)

Hidden Fears, 1991 (screenplay, from Kaminsky's novel
Exercise in Terror)

Frequence Meurtre, 1988 (story, from Kaminsky's novel ***When the Dark Man Calls***)

Enemy Territory, 1987 (story and co-screenplay)

A Woman in the Wind, 1987 (screenplay)

Once Upon a Time in America, 1983 (dialogue writer)

Any fool can make a rule and every fool will follow it.
—Henry David Thoreau

Fuck structure and grab your characters by the time balls.
—Jack Kerouac

Writing is finally play, and there is no reason why you should get paid for playing. If you're a real writer, you write no matter what. No writer need feel sorry for himself if he writes and enjoys the writing, even if he doesn't get paid for it.
—Irwin Shaw, *Writers at Work, 5th Series*

Five Queasy Pieces

When I founded and chaired the reorganization of UCLA's screenwriting program, I brought in two new screenwriting teachers, first Richard Walter and then Lew Hunter, both talented, professional screenwriters. (It has been my long-held conviction that screenwriting is best taught by working screenwriters.) Walter and Hunter, who now co-chair the screenwriting program, have proven themselves to be highly qualified teachers, building the program to its premier status.

Since my retirement, both writers have written highly successful books on screenwriting. Walter's and Hunter's books each lay out the fundamentals with clarity, and each brings his own vision to his work. Walter stresses the need for writers to understand that they are writing for an audience, and brings intelligent wit to his observations. Hunter is more didactic and a touch too pious and pompous for me.

Of my two former colleagues' books, my personal choice is Walter's. Although I agree with much of what Hunter has to say, there are some disturbing aspects of his work, one of which I am compelled to address here: Hunter claims that aspiring screenwriters may see many movies, but they need have "a viewing relationship with a mere five movies," presumably to understand the art of screenwriting. His "fantastic five" (as he calls them) are *Citizen Kane*, *Casablanca*, *E.T.*, *Butch Cassidy and the Sundance Kid*, and *Fallen Angel*, a good TV movie that Hunter wrote in 1981.

Hunter's five-movie theory is, as the basis of building a screenwriting career, just plain silly. Focusing your attention on just five, ten, or even fifteen films is errant nonsense. Imagine the Julliard School of Music telling its music composition students that they need study only five pieces of music to learn the fundamentals of composing. Or picture the art department of any major university telling its art majors that they need have a "viewing relationship" with only five paintings to learn the fundamentals of art! It's a gimmick, and a poor one at that. If you follow Hunter's silly suggestion, you will certainly stunt your growth as a screenwriter and cripple your career.

You must see as many movies as you possibly can and *make each and every one a learning experience*. It is absolutely essential that anyone aspiring to become a film professional see—and study—many, many movies in order to be current with their art and/or craft. Every film-industry meeting you will have will include brief discussions and passing references to dozens of movies, with comments about why each movie worked or didn't work. Every industry or business expects those who are employed in it to seriously understand and care about the field they work in. When auto workers get together, they discuss cars, all kinds of cars, foreign and domestic. Architects talk architecture, musicians talk music.

During my twenty-five-plus years of teaching screenwriting (at USC, UCLA, the University of Hawaii, Florida State University, Danmarks Radio, or wherever else in the world I taught screenwriting), I made it my business to be able to participate in or to lead the discussion of *any* movie that any student brought to attention of the other students. I made it my business to see at least 100 movies a year, sometimes 150, and I saw almost all of them in movie theaters.

As someone who aspires to a film career, you'd damn well better study lots of films. If you are not film literate, if you have a narrow and limited working knowledge of movies, and aren't interested enough to develop film literacy, find another occupation that will seize your attention. There are no short cuts in life and certainly not in screenwriting.

Hunter is a good writer, and I suppose his intention was to make learning screenwriting seem as easy as possible. It's tempting to look for short cuts, simpler, easier ways. Studying five movies at home on videotape, as Hunter proposes, is a hell of a lot easier than going out to the theater and studying five hundred. Let me assure you that there is no easy way to become a screenwriter and make your way into that highly competitive world. Those few who make it make it the hard way—by working at it. Until overnight screenwriting stardom comes along, you're simply going to have to do your homework, put in the hours, make a serious commitment, become knowledgeable, become professional.

Hunter's intentions are understandable, but I deplore his simplistic means of getting there. Short cuts are just another in a long list of ways to self-destruct.

How and Where to See a Movie

Go to movie theaters as often as possilbe to see movies where and how they were meant to be seen. Seeing a movie on videotape is better than not seeing it at all, but it's a terribly poor substitute. You entirely miss the moviegoing experience.

People who work in film are filmgoers. They love movies: There is something special about going out to the movies, and the whole world knows it. That is precisely why, in spite of its pervasive global popularity, television has not killed the public's desire to go to the movies. Countless millions *are not sitting at home staring at the tube*. In spite of higher prices, more people worldwide are going to the movies than ever before. It is no coincidence that an estimated *two billion people* watch the Academy Award ceremonies on Oscar night.

As an aspiring screenwriter, it is important that you get a feel for the audience, discover how the people with whom you are sharing the experience are responding to various aspects of a film: What gets a laugh? How big a laugh? Where do you become conscious of a tense silence from the crowd? What is holding their attention? Getting a feel for audience response is a very important part of your education. In fact, it's vital. After the movie, make a point of discussing its screenplay with your companion(s). There are valuable lessons in these conversations.

Like it or not, you are in the audience business. You will learn much less as a couch potato.

(Of course, when viewing the older classics, you will probably have to see them on videotape or laser disc. But this method of studying movies should always be your second option. When you must view movies on a television screen, invite writer friends to join you so that you can conduct a running discussion of the screenplay as you watch. And avoid watching movies on commercial-laden channels, where they are butchered and chopped up like sausage. This is a waste of your time.)

At the Movies

Okay, let's imagine you're in the theater. Finally, after seemingly endless trailers, pitches for candy bars, cokes, popcorn, and maybe even a few commercials, here come the main titles underscored by music. *Immediately*, you know what? The genre—the kind of movie it's going to be.

At this point, I hope you're realizing that that's exactly what your screenplay must also do. Page one, line one, sets the genre. The readers of your script must *immediately* know what kind of movie they are reading. (Just as the audience must *immediately* know what kind of movie they are watching.) Knowing the genre at once helps put your script readers in an appropriate mindset. The readers of your screenplay are your first audience; strike out with them and you're dead meat.

You are no ordinary member of the audience if you are an aspiring screenwriter. *You are in school from the moment the film begins.* From that moment on, you are making mental notes as you watch the movie. Your job now is to focus your attention on the screenplay, while also noting audience response. Make a conscious effort to ignore the camera angles, the direction, even the nuances of the performances.

As you study each movie, make mental notes on: (a) How soon do you know what the story is about and what the problem is going to be? (b) How soon do you feel dramatic tension and what is causing you to feel that way? (c) How soon are you aware of a story line, or an action line? (d) How much information is withheld, and how does that help you remain attentive to the movie? (Pay particular attention to the surprises in the story; having surprises in your stories is vital to your success.) (e) The dialogue: In particular, what is left unsaid and what is implied? What is the sub-text of the dialogue? What's going on beneath the surface? Is this an open story or a closed story?

You'll always learn more by spending your money going to the movies, and studying them, than you will paying to hear some so-called "story-structure guru" dish out the crap. Going to the movies is the way the great screenwriters learned screenwriting. They built on what was written before them. And so can you . . . at the movies.

If some pedant wants to come along after your film is made and explain to the suckers how it was constructed, step by step by step, by all means let them. (But I wonder why these gurus, with their magic formulas and secrets of screenwriting success, aren't selling multi-million-dollar screenplays.) Meanwhile, you're busy writing your next screenplay. If you want a successful career in any field of endeavor, you have to work at it—it will not be handed to you on a silver platter. Becoming a professional screenwriter is not only difficult, it is complex. Simple-minded short cuts will get you only one result: You will spend your time looking for work, instead of achieving a professional film-writing career.

You're Never Too Young

One day, a graduate screenwriting student dropped by my UCLA office to make an announcement: "My agent called to tell me that Warners likes my screenplay and wants to meet with me. Then my agent asked me how old I was. I said, 'Twenty-four,'" he continued, "and he said, 'Tell 'em you're twenty-two.'"

The story illustrates the truism that you can never be too young for Hollywood.

Hollywood's infatuation with youth stems from their research findings that young people are the movies' prime audience, and that they will go to see movies they like again and again. Ergo, according to the studio execs, it follows that only young people can write what young people will pay to see. Drawing this to its logical conclusion, only middle-aged writers can write about middle-aged people and only old writers can write stories about old people, etc. But Hollywood doesn't take it to its logical conclusion, because it's sheer nonsense to begin with. Still, they want young, young, young, because young is new, new, new.

Hollywood's antipathy to older writers has been well documented. If you're over forty, you're over the hill as far as Tinsel Town is concerned. And if you're over sixty, you may still be vertical and vital, but you're professionally dead as far as the film and television industry is concerned.

The fear of growing older is endemic in the Hollywood scene. Among some of its denizens, it reaches panic proportions and induces serious breakdowns and dangerous depressions. Not only stars have face-lifts, tummy tucks, and wrinkle surgery. I've known more than one top-ranked, past-middle-aged male screenwriter who had a face-lift. Just For Men probably sells as much hair coloring in the film capital as anywhere in the world, and plenty of it goes to screenwriters.

I know middle-aged producers who hire young assistants, as vice presidents of their companies, whose primary function is to attend studio and network meetings in order to present a more youthful front. The twenty-somethings are window dressing. Older screen-writers have taken on young "partners" to present a young image in meetings. The "partnership" may be in name only, but for the young-ster it's a great opportunity to become known, to meet important people while the older writer gets to continue his or her career be-yond its usual Hollywood lifespan.

But the screenwriter has a secret weapon no other person in filmmaking has. The screenwriter puts only his or her name on the screenplay, not a biography. So the studio, producer, agent, et al. does not really know how old the writer is when they read a screenplay, unless the writer is already established in the business. Of course, there are some highly respected screenwriters with outstanding cred-its who wear their age and their Laurels (the WGA's highest honor for a distinguished screenwriting career) like a crown. They are the rare exceptions. Many older screenwriters try to get around the prob-lem by eliminating credits from their early screenwriting and televi-sion years so as not to date themselves, listing only the most recently produced work. This is a common practice.

Many years ago I was one of the founding members of the Writers Guild of America's Age Discrimination Committee. We knew there was a serious problem for older writers, but we had to document it.

The result of our in-depth survey of the membership was predictable and tragic. Hollywood wants nothing to do with writers over forty. For that matter, the survey confirmed that Hollywood is not enthusiastic about women writers, black writers, Hispanic writers, Asian writers, gay writers, any minority writers. Nobody was really surprised to learn that Hollywood is a young, white, male-dominated industry.

Hints of small changes are in the air: We have more women executives, a few more women directors, a few more minority writers, but older is still older and nothing suggests that there is any crack in the Age Barrier.

Such is the seriousness of the Over Forty And You're Out attitude in the film industry that the Age Awareness Committee has taken out ads in the Writers Guild *Journal*, which read as follows:

PRODUCERS, AGENTS, NETWORK EXECUTIVES:
Ignoring Older Writers Can Be Injurious To Your Wealth.
Ruth Prawer Jhabvala wrote *The Bostonians* at age 57. She
won a WGA and an Academy Award for *Room with a View* at
age 59. She wrote *Mr. & Mrs. Bridge* at age 63. Her screenplay *Howard's End*, written when she was 65, won a WGA
nomination and an Academy Award. She wrote *Remains of
the Day* at age 68.

—Brought to you by the Age Awareness Committee

PRODUCERS, AGENTS, NETWORK EXECUTIVES:
Ignoring Older Writers Can Be Injurious To Your Wealth.
Ronald Bass, who won an Academy Award nomination for
Rain Man at age 44, also wrote *Code Name Emerald* (age 43),
Gardens of Stone (age 44), *Sleeping with the Enemy* (age 48),
The Joy Luck Club (age 51), and *When a Man Loves a Woman*
(age 51).

—Brought to you by the Age Awareness Committee

Woody Allen: Included in his 18 Academy and/or WGA
Award wins/nominations were the following films written
after the age of 40: *Annie Hall* (age 42), *Interiors* (age 43),

Manhattan (age 44), *Broadway Danny Rose* (age 48), *Hannah and Her Sisters* (age 50), *Bullets Over Broadway* (age 58).

The ads appear regularly. I don't know if they have any impact since the screenwriters they mention are impressively credentialed and are probably dismissed as the exceptions to the general run of older screenwriters.

Still, writers' scripts are read first before the author is seen. And a great screenplay is still a great screenplay no matter whose name is on it. (Some older writers, like the blacklisted writers of the McCarthy era, have taken to putting pseudonyms on their work to escape virulent ageism.)

I suggest that the only sensible response to this madness is to write your screenplay, get it out there into the marketplace, and, if asked, lie about your age. For you beginners trying to find an agent, if you don't live in Los Angeles, you're only a voice on the phone. You can be any age you want to be. Even if you make the first cut and find yourself in the agent's office talking about marketing your screenplay, lie about your age. Try to keep it plausible. If you're forty-five, I don't suggest you attempt to pass as eighteen, but you can probably shave off eight or ten years. A few years younger helps, pathetic as that sounds. If you can, do it.

Deceptive as this is, if you are serious about making screen-writing your career, you damn well better be prepared to get down and dirty.

Age discrimination is supposedly against the law. The industry's response is, "So what?" Besides, how can you prove it? The truth is that you can't, in spite of all the solid evidence that ageism is an ongoing endemic and pernicious aspect of not only Hollywood but also the current state of our culture in America. It's a national disgrace, peculiar to the United States.

But unlike executives who are fired for being over fifty, writers have a strong, powerful, weapon: Selling your screenplay is your best revenge. If you write a great one, nobody is going to throw it out because you are "over age." They just don't want you to mention it.

To Market, To Market

Of course, we all write to make a living. A recently published screenwriting book strongly suggests that there is something tainted or unseemly about writing for money. That should certainly leave a nasty taste in the skeletal remains of William Shakespeare's mouth, and every other writer who's plied his or her art since the dawn of storytelling. In times long past, great storytellers were given food and shelter in exchange for their stories, and today, perhaps one-hundred-thousand years later, we're still telling stories for food and shelter. If there's something ignoble about making a living writing, call me *pisher*. Let's assume we're all interested in sheltering and feeding our families, and try not to feel to guilty about it.

How do you know that what you write will sell? You don't. You begin by hoping that what interests you will interest a lot of other people.

Joseph Mankiewicz, the great writer-director, once commented, following a flop he had made (*The Quiet American*), that he regretted that his taste did not happen to coincide with the taste of the American public. Yet this is the same writer-director who gave us *All About Eve*, which won Academy Awards for Best Picture and Best Director. (Years later, this same gifted artist co-wrote and co-directed 20th Century-Fox's epic, legendary disaster *Cleopatra*.)

The point is that no matter how talented you are, you are going to have some successful screenplays and some failures. Nobody has ever batted 1.000. Babe Ruth was the home-run king, who will live forever in the annals of the sport, but he was also a strikeout king.

I have always admired what the great Broadway producer-director Herman Shumlin (who for a long time was the most successful producer in the history of Broadway) said when reporters asked him, "What happens when you spend months of time and effort producing and directing a play that turns out to be an overnight flop?"

Mr. Shumlin replied, "I forgive myself."

For aspiring and professional screenwriters, this is the only attitude that will keep one's career going and one's sanity intact. This attitude accepts failure along with success and allows one to move quickly on to the next screenplay.

I wrote a screenplay that I thought might be marketable and that my agent, Frank Cooper, was quite enthusiastic about it. Yet after seemingly dozens of submissions to studios, all we got were rejections. Finally, I urged Frank to abandon it; it would become part of my learning experience. I loved that story, but no one but Frank seemed to share my enthusiasm. "Always remember," he told me, "it only takes one buyer to like it."

He persisted in submitting my "loser." And after a few more weeks, that one buyer came along. I got $50,000 for this "loser," which, in 1966, was big money.

Possibly the most exciting thing about being "in the business" is that you never know when lightening will strike . . . or when you will fall on your ass.

I have never forgotten Frank Cooper's lesson and I pass it along with the hope that you will accept its wisdom. "It only takes one buyer to like it."